THE STATE
AND
THE CITIZEN

THE STATE
AND
THE CITIZEN

bY

K. M. PANIKKAR

GYAN

Published by

GYAN

Gyan Publishing House
5, Ansari Road
Daryaganj, New Delhi-110002
Phone: 011-47034999, 9811692060
E-mail: books@gyanbooks.com

Distribution Network
gyanbooks.com
India, USA, Canada, UK, Australia

ISBN: 978-81-212-0940-3 (HB)
First Published, 1956

2nd Impression 2024

Printed at: Gyan Press, Delhi.

THE STATE AND THE CITIZEN
Author: K. M. PANIKKAR

THE STATE AND THE CITIZEN

THE STATE
AND
THE CITIZEN

by

K M PANIKKAR

ASIA PUBLISHING HOUSE
BOMBAY CALCUTTA NEW DELHI MADRAS

Contents

Introduction

The State and the Citizen

IN A DEPENDENT society, the individual is a subject. He has neither the rights nor the obligations of a citizen. He obeys the law because he is forced to do so; he performs such services and duties as he is compelled to, not because he has any obligation. In an independent state where the people govern themselves the situation is fundamentally different. The basic assumption in a free community is that each individual shares in the responsibility of government and has duties and rights towards the society and the state. The obligations of a free citizen in a self-governing community are therefore different from those imposed on him in a dependent society.

In discussing the position of the individual in regard to the state in India this is a major consideration which we must constantly keep in mind. During our struggle for independence we developed attitudes and ways of thinking appropriate to our position as a dependent people fighting to secure freedom. We were for over a quarter of a century in revolt against the state, denying its moral validity and claiming the right to disobey its laws and to force it into courses of action by methods of non-cooperation. While no one can deny that an unfree society has the right to resort to such action—in fact the right to rebel—it is obvious that such action in a self-governing society is against the fundamental postulates of freedom. Leaving alone the group of thinkers who believe in philosophical anarchism—Bakunin, Kropotkin and others—there has been practical unanimity from the time of Bhishma that a free society involved duties and obligations without which man would fall back to the law of the jungle. A widely accepted doctrine of social obedience is therefore of the essence of free society. The constitution of India lays down in general the duties and rights of the citizen, and the democratic nature of that constitution, and its processes at all levels place on each individual the responsibility of sharing in the government. It postulates the widest measure of freedom for the individual and entrusts each one with the duty of participating in the determination of such duties and obligations as are placed on him. The principle of obedience is voluntary and proceeds ultimately from the individual himself.

It is necessary to emphasise this obvious point for one of the major problems in India is the survival of the doctrine of disobedience which we had, in the unfree society of the past, adopted with every justification as a weapon of revolt. It is not an uncommon feature of life in India for individuals to go on "fasts unto death" for political purposes, for students to go on strike, for groups to reject the decisions which the government takes after due democratic processes. We have had some notable instances of such action during the last few years. It is therefore necessary to examine how far in the present state of our society such actions can be morally justified. How far is it within the rights of the citizen to disobey the law? How far is it justifiable for individuals to organise the public to resist an unpopular decision taken in full view of the public and after the ascertainment of national opinion? As the name of Mahatma Gandhi is often appealed to by the advocates of such resistance, it is necessary to consider this question carefully and in all its implications.

The right of mass disobedience is the right to revolt against a state. Such a right undoubtedly exists in the case of a dependent people, as the reduction of a people to such dependence is based generally on conquest. Though a people may have accepted subjection voluntarily, their continuance in subjection cannot be assumed to be voluntary. Freedom is the right of every society, and the deprivation of it involves the right of a people to revolt. The right of disobedience is only a passive form of the right to revolt. But does such a right exist in a free society? Normally the answer is no. If a society ceases to be free, or pursues a course of deliberate injustice to an integrated group of people, such a right may be said to arise. Assuming that, in a multiple society, one section dominates another against which it uses all the powers of the state to maintain it in subjection, then clearly the group so held down or oppressed has the right to disobey or to revolt. Mahatma Gandhi in his life emphasised both these truths. The Civil Disobedience Movement in South Africa was the assertion of the right of a section held in subjection and differentiated against by law to gain its rights by passive resistance against the state. The Non-Cooperation Movement in India was the revolt of a people against the state with the object of gaining freedom. But the problem is different when the citizens of a free society claim such a right against the state. Here again a distinction has to be made. It is the right of each individual, where his conscience is concerned, to decide whether he could submit to the authority of the state. In such a case the authority of the state is not denied, but the individual, obeying what is to him a higher law, voluntarily submits himself to punishment rather than obey an unjust law. This undoubted right in a free society should not be confused with the right to organise disobedience, for this latter involves a denial of the validity of the state's action and is a repudiation of the allegiance to the state. Such a right does not exist in a free society.

The failure to recognise this essential difference has been at the bottom of much confused thinking in India. We have, as a result of thirty years struggle, based on Civil Disobedience, come to value its irresistible potency, and we take pride in the fact that it is through this process that we won our freedom from alien rule. But many people in India seem also to think that it is an instrument which can be used against our own state. The numerous abortive satyagrahas, during the past ten years, should help us to realise that the obligations of the citizen in a free self-governing democratic state are inconsistent with the doctrine of passive resistance and the survival of this doctrine among a section of our people is an anachronism which may have dangerous consequences.

Another unfortunate survival from the period of our national struggles is the attitude of the students to authority and the support that public men extend to student action. In no free society has one heard of students' strikes. In England, America, France, or any of the other free countries, do the students claim the right to walk out of educational institutions? In India, in Egypt and in the past in Kuomintang China widespread student activity in politics and withdrawal from colleges for alleged grievances were common features. Again it is a survival of the doctrines of our political struggle. When a nation is engaged in the fight for freedom it is entitled to call upon its young men to join the national struggle. In the same way as compulsory military service was extended to university students during the two great wars and colleges were denuded of their members in European countries, the nation had the undoubted right of calling on the youth of the country to participate in the fight for freedom. But again the persistence of the idea that the students have the right to strike and to carry on agitation is a projection of our past methods into a free society. The right to strike is based on the idea of conflicting interests. In a competitive society, unorganised workers are generally recognised as having a right to strike to secure justice to themselves. But it is necessary to emphasise that in non-capitalist societies this right does not exist, and even in capitalist societies there are strict limitations to its exercise. Clearly the relationship of the students to the university is not that of the employed and the employer. No conflict of interests can be presumed to exist between them as the university exists solely for the students. The right to strike against the university would therefore seem to be meaningless and the support that such action on the part of the students receives from political leaders can only be considered as an unfortunate survival of our past attitudes.

In a modern society the right of the citizen in relation to the state is the most complicated of all problems. Every state in the world today is totalitarian, in the sense that it claims the totality of powers. It was said in the beginning of the century that the modern state was Jenghiz Khan with the telegraph line. Today it is much more than that. It is Jenghiz Khan with distance control exercised by a hundred methods. It speaks with a million voices on the radio. It overhears our conversations on the telephone. It prys into our secret thoughts by censoring our letters. It controls the water we drink, the food we eat, the lights we use, our modes of transportation, and in fact practically everything in our lives. It gives with one hand and takes away with the other. In fact its picture is that of some demon of Hindu mythology multiplied manifold, a Ravana with a thousand faces and a million hands, each hand wielding a different instrument of power. What chance has the individual against such an institution—impersonal, all-pervasive, unmoved by sentiment, armed both by the power of the law and by every possible instrument of authority. The individual in the modern state, whether it be capitalist or communist, is reduced to a position of nullity.

And yet, all this concentration of power is said to be in the interests of the individual himself. And to a large extent this is true. The *laissez-faire* tradition of liberalism on which the doctrine of individual liberty is based and to which we hark back did not lead to an Arcadian system of happiness. It meant inevitably the right of the capitalist to exploit the worker, of the powerful to oppress the weak, of the rich to grow richer, and the poor to grow poorer, all in the sacred name of the liberty of the individual. It was the doctrine of the devil taking the hindmost. Life was conceived as a race for success with the state, heavily over-weighted in favour of privilege, as the umpire. It is the omnipotent state that has set right some of these injustices of a competitive society by emphasising the ideals of economic equality, social security, nationalised health services, organisation of labour to prevent exploitation, control of production and distribution in order to secure for everyone the minimum necessities of good living. It is only an omnipotent state which claims the right to act in every sphere that can be a welfare state. When all this is said, the problem still remains of safeguarding the position of the individual in the modern state. This is the fundamental contradiction in free societies today. In India we are facing this at every turn. The tradition of British administration in India was necessarily one of *laissez-faire*. It tried, except where its own security was concerned, to avoid interference with Indian life and was content to leave us to ourselves—a doctrine which led Mahatma Gandhi to exclaim that of all governments he had the least objection to the British government as it governed the least. But with independence the situation has undergone a revolutionary change. Our objective is the creation of a welfare state based on economic and social planning. By its very nature, it has to interfere with all aspects of our life; even with such intimate things as family relationships, marriage and inheritance, not to speak of the complete control it has claimed over our economic activities. Such a development was necessary and unavoidable. The problem is how to reconcile these claims with the rights of the individual.

The Indian Constitution in a measure realised the significance of this problem and incorporated in the Fundamental Law a chapter affirming and guaranteeing the basic rights of the citizen. This declaration of Fundamental Rights is a self-denying act by the state itself in favour of the individual. Feedom of expression, conscience, assembly etc., to which the Liberal State attached importance are secured to us by the constitution and so far the state has worked within that rigid framework. And yet nowhere has legal protection been sufficient to safeguard human rights. It is only by constant vigilance by the public itself that the inevitable tendency of the state to encroach on the rights of the individual can be checked. It is here that India has been slack. Instances can be quoted both at the Centre and in the States where such invasions on the rights of the individual have been accepted without protest. One case deserves special mention. A distinguished writer of Indian origin, Mr. Aubrey Menen, published in England a satirical work entitled *Rama Retold* in which he dealt in an unorthodox manner with the characters of Rama and Sita. The book did not attract wide attention in India, but the Government of India, considering it objectionable, prohibited its entry into India and forfeited all copies already imported. The reason alleged was that the book was likely to wound the susceptibilities of the Hindus who looked upon Rama as an Avatar of God. It is not necessary for the purpose of our discussion to discuss the validity of this argument, though it may be noted *en passant* that much more virulent criticism of Rama is common enough in the books produced in Southern India, and that at the very time that *Rama Retold* was being proscribed a more offensive parody of the Rama story was being widely circulated in Madras. Also it is worthy of note that it is a part of the general tradition of Hinduism to criticise the worldly activities of Avatars, a notable instance being the attitude of the early Arya Samaj writers to the Krishna legend. It may be that the Home Ministry was justified in the action it took on the grounds of public security and the maintenance of law and order. But the point here is that the action of the government passed practically unnoticed and was not subjected to any criticism in India itself. The lack of public interest in the maintenance of public rights is a danger signal in democracy, for we should never forget Jefferson's wise dictum that the only safe depositaries of the rights of the people are the people themselves.

Another important duty of an intelligent citizen is to resist the influence of mass opinion on his mind. This is particularly important in a democracy where the mass-mind is quickly aroused and is often unscrupulously led. In monarchies dynastic interests, and in oligarchies the vested interests of groups, stand in the way of such exploitation of mass-opinion. The history of modern states proves clearly that in communities where leadership is based on public opinion the tendency to exploit mass-emotions is almost irresistible. What divides democracy from tyranny is but a thin line; and this line is the toleration of unpopular opinions. All democracies have a tendency to equate unpopular opinion with anti-state and unpatriotic activity. It shows itself in a hundred apparently inoffensive ways in normal times; but in times of crisis it develops into a national hysteria, and those who hold unpopular opinions are branded as enemies of the people. Even in England, where toleration of unpopular opinion is a part of the national tradition, the difficulties that Lord Landsdowne, a former Foreign Secretary, encountered for expressing the view that a negotiated peace may perhaps be desirable, the persecution to which Bertrand Russell was subjected for holding unpopular views in regard to war, and the way Ramsay MacDonald was treated during the first Great War should make us realise that, in times of national hysteria, democracies are especially subject to this danger. In new democracies where the tradition of tolerance in political matters is not strong, it is therefore particularly important that we should not merely emphasise the right to free speech, but uphold as a matter of national importance the right to the free expression of unpopular opinion. This is in fact what freedom of speech means. The danger is an insidious one for, generally, it is not through government action that unpopular opinion gets suppressed, but through the action of the public itself. It is therefore a primary duty of the individual citizen to see that democracy does not get debased into tyranny by insistence on conformity, by denying expression to views against the current of popular opinion. The famous declaration of Voltaire, that he would fight to death a certain opinion but that he would equally fight to death for the right to maintain such an opinion, represents the true democratic spirit. This is a point of view that cannot be too strongly emphasised in a modern society which shows unusual readiness to accept mass-judgement on vital matters, especially when the propagation of mass-judgement is aided by the most modern techniques, the radio, the cinema and the tabloid press.

We have so far dealt with the problem of safeguarding the individual's rights in a modern democratic state. Equally basic to the conception of democracy is the individual's duty of participation in the working of the state. The sovereignty being vested in the people, the ultimate responsibility of all action rests with them. This is emphasised to some extent by the system of elections based on adult franchise to all governing bodies, parliaments, assemblies, district boards, municipalities, etc. But the citizen's duty does not cease with his voting at elections and then leaving the work of governance to the leaders thus chosen, or to those who make a profession of politics. For the people to wake up at election times and then again go to sleep is to allow the forms of democracy to be utilised by interested groups. More than that, it is not an efficient or satisfactory way of government. Democracy can function satisfactorily only if there is constant and unceasing cooperation between the public and the government. It is only by the cooperative thinking of thousands of people working through voluntary organisations that ideas and policies are formulated in a democratic state. It is the widespread existence of such organisations, academic, voluntary, functional, at political, social and economic levels that provides the necessary background of ideas for a democratic government. Whether organised by parties, or by independent groups, such cooperative thinking on essential issues is what provides both the framework of criticism and the machinery for independent thought in a modern state. Thus trade unions, chambers of commerce, research institutions, academic conferences, not to speak of specialised bodies devoting themselves to the examination of social and political questions, are equally the organs of the democratic state as are the more formal institutions like parliaments and other legislative bodies. Unless the citizens of a state take continuous interest in the development of ideas and their popularisation, democracy cannot function as a dynamic political system.

A special duty rests on the citizens to ensure that the declared purposes of the state are not ignored and overlooked by political leaders. The modern state exists to fulfil certain defined social and economic purposes, for the steady pursuit of certain ideals. We in India have defined them in our Constitution where emphasis is laid on social justice as the objective of the state. We have further elaborated it as the achievement of a welfare state based on a socialist pattern. Now, it is obvious that in every society, however progressive, there will be powerful elements which, under different pretexts, will be trying to weaken these purposes if not actively to oppose them; forces of social reaction, basing themselves on a veneration of the past, forces representing communal or economic privilege, speaking the language of stability and security. It is the duty of the citizen to be vigilant with regard to these forces and to show awareness of the dangers inherent in such developments.

A more insidious danger lurks in the possibility of the leadership in the country becoming complacent and losing the sense of dynamism. The great urges and motivations which carried us forward during the period of national struggle may be weakened by time. This is a common enough phenomenon in politics and the history of new nations provides many instances of a gradual weakening of national purposes. The most conspicuous examples in modern times are those of the Kuomintang in China, and of the Wafd in Egypt. This inherent danger can only be counteracted by the active interest of the vast mass of citizens in the policies of the state, their constant vigilance against back-sliding and continuous and unremitting pressure against any weakening of the national will. It is only where there are widespread and intelligent groups of citizens, who by criticism and constant watchfulness keep the leadership up to the mark, that a democracy functions as a progressive social structure.

There is only one other tendency to which I shall allude here. In Asian countries, especially, there is a tendency to elevate the leader to a position of unique importance and invest him almost with superhuman virtues. This may be described as the "father conception", a phenomenon which becomes specially noticeable if the leadership remains continuously in the same hands over a long period. This may be seen in practically every country in Asia. One result of this development is that the leader remains above criticism, his actions, his attitudes and his prejudices being taken as something sacrosanct. We have recently seen how this "father principle" operated even in the Soviet Union and how the Soviet leaders had to wait for some time to elapse before the myth of the great Stalin, "the inspired leader and the teacher of humanity", could first be quietly given up and then publicly attacked. The danger of the development of the conception of the unique leader is no less great in Asia's new democracies. It is our good fortune that, so far as India is concerned, Mahatma Gandhi, though reverenced and almost worshipped by the masses, was so firm in his faith in democratic processes as to submit himself to public criticism and often to withdraw from leadership. This is even more true of Pandit Nehru. In spite of the unexampled adulation of the people, and the unique authority he has established in the country, he has himself fought against the growth of the "leadership principle" and helped actively to develop in India collective responsibility and free criticism. But the trends are there among the people and it is the duty of every citizen to be constantly on guard against them.

Democracy is a system which in normal times requires dispersed leadership for its success. Only in exceptional circumstances does it require unique leadership which concentrates power in its own hands. In times of crises, it not only tolerates but welcomes the leadership of the exceptional individual—a Churchill, a Roosevelt, or a de Gaulle; but in normal circumstances it frowns upon such people—Aristides the Just is rewarded in democracy by exile; and a Churchill, who led the nation with heroic greatness during a life and death struggle, is defeated in an election at the end of the crisis. In India, the circumstances of our new freedom required an exceptional leader in whom the powers of the state could be concentrated. It was our good fortune that the leader was one whose burning faith in democracy ensured us against the development of a system of veiled dictatorship, using the form of democracy for the maintenance of an authoritarian regime. But the future is something which depends on the people themselves and it is the duty of every citizen to be vigilant about it.

In the addresses included in this volume, I have tried to discuss some of the problems which face the new generation in India. Though they do not constitute a connected work, there is, I hope, a central unity in so far as each one of these papers deals with some aspect of the individual's relationship to society in general and to the state in particular. It is in the belief that the problems raised in these addresses deserve to be discussed that I have ventured to publish them as a book.

21st March, 1956 K. M. PANIKKAR

Poverty and National Welfare

IT IS A matter of special gratification to me, in view of the great kindness which Gurudeva* extended to me over a fairly long period, that you should have invited me to be your Chief Guest at your annual celebrations and to deliver the Convocation Address to the graduates of the Visva-Bharati this year. This institution which is the gift of Gurudeva to the Indian people is one which is dear to every true lover of modern India, for it seeks to enshrine the great ideals which the Poet preached in his life and to which he awakened his people by his own life and activities. One of the most important of his contributions to the life of modern India is the fact that he made India conscious of her place in Asia. By his historic visits to Indonesia, China and Japan he inaugurated a new era of Asian co-operation, and was the undoubted pioneer of a great movement which is having far reaching results today. In this matter it can justly be claimed that he was the successor in our time of Kumarajiva, Kashyapa Matanga, Vajrabodhi, Buddha Ghosha and the rest of the galaxy of saints and scholars who, in an earlier age, established, on a firm basis, the intellectual and cultural relationship between India and the other countries of Asia. Wherever he went he carried with him the message of India; and when he returned he brought with him a firmer conviction of the necessity of co-operation between nations. And this great institution bears witness to that spirit of intellectual adventure,

Address to the Visva-Bharati, 1955.

* Gurudeva means revered teacher: here it stands for the poet Tagore, who was generally addressed as Gurudeva at Visva-Bharati.

for here he was able to provide ample facilities for the study of Asian culture such as exist in but few institutions in the world. It is a great heritage that the Gurudeva has left to us, and it is for us to uphold that tradition of tolerance and universality which, in the true spirit of Indian culture, he emphasised by his own life and by his teachings.

For, let us not forget the great truth which he taught us that the true tradition of India is one which welcomed, assimilated and made its own what was best in the culture of other countries. Today, however, one notices a tendency, arising no doubt from a false sense of nationalism, to forget this great aspect of Indian tradition and to emphasise the self-sufficiency of Indian culture and to try and build our future on a perverted view of our past. Recently a very distinguished friend of mine pressed on the Commission of which I was a member, that India should be organised on the basis of the *Tapovans* (forest retreats) of the past, each under a dedicated sage, living a life of contemplation, or, as he expressed it, practising simple living and high thinking. I do not know whether at any time life in India was organised on the basis of forest retreats. All historical evidence disproves it, for we know that, at all times, a vigorous urban life existed in India and the *Tapovans,* where they existed, were few and far between. Even today such *Tapovans* exist and this great university is a modern version of it. But could anything be more fantastic than the idea that our political structure should be a collection of *Tapovans*, isolated communities, practising austerities and no doubt engaged in the contemplation of the Absolute.

The idea of a return to the villages and to the simplicity of a handicraft economy is but a variation of the same theme. Nobody would deny the importance of the village in Indian life. Nor is anyone likely to contest the claims of handicrafts, which embody so much of artistic tradition and of individual craftsmanship and skill, to a place in national economy. What the Sriniketan has done in this connection is a shining example of fruitful national effort for the preservation and encouragement of handicrafts. But this is not what the advocates of village economy desire. They deny the values of an urban civilisation and claim that only by going back to a simpler life, a life of abstinence and reduction of wants, could India be true to herself. This seems to me a very strange and reactionary proposition. The self-sufficient villages of India, as indeed of all primitive communities, for instance the Russian *mirs*, were the result of an absence of communications. When communities lived apart without easy methods of transportation they had, as far as possible, to be self-sufficient. But today, with the development of communications, the village economy of the past has broken down beyond recovery. The recognition of this major development is the basis of our community projects and national extension services. They take as their unit, not a single village, but a much larger group, trying to integrate the economic and welfare activities of a whole area, thereby repudiating the doctrine of village self-sufficiency.

When we come to the question of handicrafts, which many people desire to see elevated as our basic national effort of development, the situation is even more strange. Most handicrafts in India are based on occupational castes. Where the tradition is vigorous and contributes to national economy, it deserves no doubt to be encouraged; but let us not forget that to attempt to revive dying industries is to uphold and strengthen the system of caste, which everyone agrees must be rooted out if India is to progress.

The doctrine of the simple life which is presumed to encourage high thinking is but the worship of poverty. Voluntary poverty is indeed a great thing and the ideal of the renunciation of wants on which alone it could be based is something which the world has respected at all times. But to accept poverty as a national ideal is something which is totally absurd. At no time in India was this preached as an ideal. The Vedic hymns are prayers for more and more wealth. All the descriptions which have come down to us of life in ancient India, except of course of the *rishis* living in isolated *Tapovans,* show the emphasis on economic prosperity and even on personal luxury. Even the *Saptarishis*, the supreme examples of renunciation, are described by Kalidasa as being clothed in gold and wearing sacred threads of pearls. All Hindu gods and goddesses, except of course Shiva, are pictured in the greatest luxury. The idea that the Hindu religion supports the doctrine of simple living seems to me to be wholly untrue.

In any case, this worship of poverty is a false creed. It was no more than a vague escapism in the days of our national poverty. But today, when the effort of the nation is directed towards greater production of wealth and its better distribution so that every one can have a richer life, this exaltation of poverty is something anti-social, which the good sense of our people will, I am convinced, reject absolutely.

We are also being continuously warned that this desire to increase production would usher in materialism, would lead to the exaltation of life in this world. We are told that such a development would lead to the ruin of India's spirituality, whatever it may mean, which it is claimed is the special greatness of our country. This claim of spirituality deserves some examination. On what is India's claim to greater spirituality than the rest of the world based? Is it on the ground that her thinkers in the past devoted themselves to metaphysical enquiries more than to the better ordering of society?, or again, Is it on the ground that greatness in the world was measured not by worldly achievement, but by spiritual attainment? On either of these grounds, it appears to me that the claim of India to be more spiritual than the rest of the world is no more than a self-deception. Even assuming that the ancient seers of the Vedas and the Upanishads had attained greater spiritual heights and that the store of wisdom in our sacred books is greater, unless it is a fact that our life is ordered on the basis of that wisdom, and the conduct of man, by and large, in India is guided by those spiritual qualities, it cannot be maintained that India is more spiritually-minded than others. If philosophical thought, apart from activity, is the guide, then Europe can claim to be as spiritual on the basis of Christian teachings as India is or claims to be. Other-worldliness and spiritual life are preached as much in the Sermon on the Mount as in our sacred books. If it is claimed that the difference is that while Europe does not live up to her Christian ideals India cherishes her spiritual ideals, I think the argument is altogether misleading. Nowhere in fact is materialism so rampant as in India, nowhere is the struggle for existence more rigorous, nowhere do worldliness and the desire for advantage over others have a greater hold on the people than in India. In fact, whatever the scriptures might have preached and exceptional individuals practised, the hold of materialism on India has always been as great as in other countries.

If the argument in favour of our greater spirituality is that we show honour and respect for those who have given up worldly advancement, surely this is equally true of the peoples of Europe. One has only to look at the imposing list of saints in the Christian Church, men who renounced the world for the practice of spiritual discipline, to realise that such men and women are as much honoured in the West, as in India.

And what is the alleged materialism of the West? Any serious study of Western life would convince the enquirer that, side by side with a desire for material prosperity, there exist in the West a spirit of disciplined service, a desire to further the well-being of mankind as a whole and a deep sensitiveness to suffering and misery born of a profound humanism, which constitute a unique translation of the religion of the spirit in practical life. In the Western countries in general one sees, both inside the organised churches and outside them, an immense amount of selfless activity—true *Nishkama karma*—disciplined, directed and purposeful—for the moral welfare of the world. Has present-day "spiritual" India anything to compare with the great Orders of the Catholic Church—men and women reeruited from all classes of society, vowed to chastity, poverty and a hard life, who are spread in different corners of the world dedicating their lives to the service of their fellow men? Has India anything to compare with the beneficient activity of the lay societies in Western countries which found hospitals, fight epidemics and other scourges like leprosy, tuberculosis and cancer? Could these selfless activities—voluntary, enthusiastic and continuous—be carried on by people who are alleged to be worshipping Mammon and pursuing with single-minded zeal the materialistic end of their own individual happiness?

Further, this desire to a return to a pure Indian way of life, based on *Tapovans*, village self-sufficiency and handicraft economics, based on the assumption that a life so ordered will be in the true tradition of spiritual India, is itself meaningless as the life of new India is already based on other principles. Even a casual observer of the social, economic and political life in India can see that India is no longer merely the inheritor of the thought of India's own past. What India today represents is the emergence of a new civilisation and not merely the continuation of an old one.

In the New India which we are trying to build up this doctrine of past glory and this desire to return to the village to live a life of alleged simplicity seems altogether inappropriate, for the inheritance that India has stepped into is only partly Hindu and Indian. The inheritance from the West is no less important in many fields. Modern India does not live under the laws of Manu. Her mental background and equipment, though largely influenced by the persistence of Indian tradition, have been moulded into their present shape by over a hundred years of Western education, extending practically to every field of mental activity. Its social ideals are not what Hindu society had for long cherished, but those assimilated from the West and derived predominantly from the teachings of Western social thinkers. Even the religious beliefs of Hinduism have been transformed substantially during the course of the last one hundred years. In fact it will be no exaggeration to say that the New Indian State represents traditions, ideals and principles which are the results of an effective, even if imperfect, synthesis between the East and the West.

The quality of civilisation, as Mr. R. H. Tawney has stated, depends on the transmission less of physical qualities than of a complex structure of habits, knowledge and beliefs. Modern India has inherited along with its own four thousand years of history, and the habits, thoughts and beliefs coming down through ages, a not inconsiderable measure of ideals, knowledge and thought rooted in the two thousand five hundred years of European history. It is not only through direct inheritance that these have now become a part of Indian tradition. It is to a large extent through the modifications that these ideas have forced on the thoughts, habits and beliefs of the Indian people themselves that Europe has passed into India.

The social reformation in Hindu society, the rise of the untouchable classes, the profoundly significant purification of Hinduism, all of which are of greater and more permanent significance than even the emergence of India as an independent State, are the outward reflections of that Western inheritance. The organisation of the democratic state, its secular character, the structure of its institutions and the political principles underlying them are also essentially European in their inspiration.

The tradition of India has always been one of synthesis. Her geographical position perhaps helped her to develop a singular ability to absorb the culture of others and assimilate it without losing her own identity. It is the synthesis of the Aryan and Dravidian that laid the basis of Hindu civilisation. The unity of India in her primary institutions, the village, the family, the broad legal conceptions of property, was the outcome of that synthesis. The great Gandhara school of art has definite and identifiable Greek characteristics, and the collaboration between the peoples of Bactria and the Indian borderlands is seen also in the notable advances of astronomy and mathematics in the Gupta era. The prolonged contact with Islam had, as we know, profound significance for every aspect of Indian life, religion, literature, art and social organisation and economic structure. This co-operative attitude towards what comes from outside enabled India, during the last 150 years, to accept as her own and assimilate the knowledge and thought of Europe to an extent which has enabled her to adjust herself to the new world without undergoing a violent revolution. A meeting-ground of the East and the West claiming spiritual kinship with both, India is historically well-fitted for evolving a new society based on the synthesis of Europe and Asia.

A retired Anglo-Indian administrator, Lord Meston, compared the influence of the West on India to a river flowing into the sea. "There has been nothing, or very little," he says "of clash between her own ancient culture and the alien culture imported from the West, no violent conflict of ideas or methods, no forcible replacement of one social system by another. The more fitting metaphor would be that of a stream of new thought and practice flowing into the sea of India's traditions and life. We can trace, for a time at least, the distinctive colour of the river, spreading out over the surface of the sea; but as we have often cause to reflect in India, how little can we tell of its influence in the ocean depth beneath."

While it is possible to exaggerate the influence of the West on India, the view that holds that the changes which have resulted from the contact between India and Europe have only touched the fringes of society, or merely added a veneer to it is basically wrong, primarily because it does not take into account the transformations that have taken place and the forces that have been set in motion within the apparent calmness of Indian life.

It is not true that there has been no clash between India's culture and the culture of the West. It is also not true that there have been no violent conflicts of ideas and methods. What is true is that these clashes and conflicts were carried on inside Hinduism and away from the view of India's alien masters. They have not led to violence in the physical sense of forcible breaking down of institutions, of orthodoxy and heterodoxy fighting open battles, leading to loss of life. But compulsion through the sense of danger to national existence, through the growth of moral opinion, through the threat of large-scale conversions to Islam and Christianity, there was in all the major changes that have altered what at one time were considered the special characteristics of Hindu civilisation, e.g. the caste system, the joint family, the segregation of untouchables, early marriage of women, etc.

Observant Indian leaders have at all times recognised and given credit to this transformation of ancient Indian culture as being essentially the result of Western impacts. Mr. Gopal Krishna Gokhale, the greatest statesman of his time in India and a profound student of social changes, declared at the Universal Races Conferences in London in 1911 that, "whereas the contact of the West with other countries had only been external, in India, the West had so to say entered into the very bone and marrow of the East."

No one realised this with greater force, or bewailed it more, than the champions of orthodoxy who were reduced to the position of impotent spectators when the institutions to which they attached religious sanction and which they revered as "eternal" were, one after the other, quietly given up, publicly denounced or legally destroyed; for instance when the Civil Marriage Act cut the very roots of caste, when the joint family slowly decayed and gave way, when the temples were thrown open to the untouchables and widows were permitted to remarry.

If, as I firmly believe, it is true that a new civilisation, rooted firmly in our past but assimilating the thought and achievements of the modern world, is being developed in India, then the primary duty of our young men is to strengthen it, give it greater content, extend its scope and make it a living force, at all levels of our society. This is the charge that is laid on the next generation and I have not the least doubt that the graduates of the Visva-Bharati University, trained and brought up as they are in an atmosphere of international co-operation and inheriting the burning faith of its founder in a universal civilisation which incorporates the best in all cultures, will never forget his message and will carry on vigorously the fight for a New Life in this country.

The life of man is not only in the material world, but also in the world of ideas, which, even if he does not create them, he shares with others, in a social and cultural environment which he has mostly inherited. In India today we live in two such worlds at the same time, a world of ideas which we share with the rest of the civilised world, and another world which, in part unconsciously and in part consciously, we have inherited from our past. We believe in individual freedom; but we also pay passive tribute to astrology and the strange belief that stars determine our course of action. We believe in the material truth of this world, but also talk of *maya*. We emphasise more and more the necessity of better conditions in this life, but also believe that the true rewards of *karma* are in the next life. This life in two worlds, this acceptance of contradictory ideas, gives an air of unreality to the conditions in India.

The dualism in our society is equally embarrassing. Even while we believe in progressive social principles and are actively engaged in introducing reforms in our social structure, the overwhelming influence of our inherited social institutions on the individuals is a fact which should be obvious to everyone. For example, even when we do not believe in caste most of us go on performing our caste *samskaras*. Even if we believe in civil marriage, we prefer to go through ancient ceremonies. Society is slow to change, and though cumulatively the changes that have taken place and are taking place in India are fundamental and will in time transform our society, the contradictions which are apparent today convey an impression of uncertainty which obscures the great changes that have already taken place.

Apart from the composite nature of our new civilisation, it should be remembered that we are living in an age of what may be called a cosmic disturbance in the world of ideas. The tide of knowledge is sweeping away much of what was considered fundamental in the past. Not only that, but as a great historian has stated: "In times of such cosmic disturbance the historic process attains suddenly an enormous speed: developments that otherwise need ages, seem to proceed in months, even in weeks." We have only to look round to see how profoundly true this statement is. As a result of an unprecedented advance in scientific knowledge during the last few decades, we are now compressing within a period of years what it would have taken centuries in the normal course of evolution. Consequently every aspect of our life is undergoing change, without our being even aware of it sometimes. The peasant in his farm, even if he has no notion of the scientific advances of today, is affected by it, no less than the worker in the factory and the professor in his study. At a period of change like this, when India is taking giant steps forward, the malignant continuance of unreason, bigotry and blind adherence to past notions, based on a perverted idea of an imaginary past, is a deadly enemy which each one of us has to fight in his own sphere.

Professor Julian Huxley in a notable affirmation of his faith has stated what a progressive society should stand for. "There is," he says "inevitably some conflict between the interests of individuals and those of society. But the conflict is in large measure transcended in this conception of man as an evolving psycho-social organism. This dictates certain conclusions. In the longest term point of view, our aim must be to develop a type of society and culture capable of ever-fresh evolution, one which continuously opens the way to newer and fuller realisations; in the medium term point of view, we must secure the reproduction and improvement of the pyscho-social organism, the maintenance of the frame-work of society and culture and their transmission in time; and in the immediate point of view, we must aim at maximum individual fulfilment." Briefly stated this means three things—continuous improvement of the social environment, the maintenance of the frame-work of society in order to enable it to transmit culture, and the fullest development of the individual within that frame-work. This is what the new civilisation in India stands for. This is what the Gurudeva taught and endeavoured to achieve in a life-time of activity. And this is the message he has left to India, which it is the duty of each one of us, but more especially of you, his direct spiritual heirs, to carry forward with a sense of mission and with a determination to realise the values he has communicated to us, both by his incomparable writings and by his practical activity in this University.

In conclusion, I can but echo what a Hebrew poet of modern times has said to the youth of his own country, a sentiment which I want every young man in India to share.

> We are of the mighty
> The last generation of slaves and the first generation of free men
> Alone our hand in its strength
> Tore from the pride of our shoulders, the yoke of bondage
> We lifted our heads to the heavens and behold their broadness
> Was narrow in the pride of our eyes
> ... ...
> With the eagles of heaven, we drink from her fountains of freedom.

Having lifted up our eyes to heaven and drunk from the fountains of freedom, it is for us to ensure that the vision abides with us. The Great Poet, who was among the first to catch that vision and communicate its beauty to us, whose imagination flew fearlessly with the eagles of heaven, demands of us that we should hold fast to that vision and transmit it to our successors. That is the duty which he laid on you, his spiritual heirs, it is to that great mission you have to be true in your life.

The Constitution

THE TWO outstanding facts which symbolise the rebirth of India as a nation are the territorial integration of our country and the democratic political structure embodied in our Constitution. The mere coming into being of a state with an area of over a million and two hundred thousand square miles and a population of over 360 millions, under a single authority, is a fact of major significance. The political unity of India from the Himalayas to Cape Comorin, from the Beas to the Brahmaputra, is an ideal which neither Asoka nor Samudra Gupta could conceive, which neither the Moghuls nor the Marathas could achieve, which the British during the century and a half of their rule could not constitutionally enforce. The writ of united India runs unquestioned in territories where neither King nor Parliament had any legal authority. Today we can claim with pride that from a geographical expression India has been converted into a nation. It is the growth of integral nationalism among the people of India which undermined the political divisions based on historical accidents, making them obsolete, meaningless and reactionary, that enabled us to achieve this result.

The unification of so large a territory and the creation of a single nation-state with so large a population would have been at all times an important event. What makes it an event of world importance is the nature of the state as expressed in the Constitution which we have evolved as a result of years of patient labour. The Government of India Act, 1935, on

Convocation of the Delhi University, 1950.

which many of the more detailed clauses of our Constitution are based, was itself the result of a co-operative effort by Indians and Englishmen for a period of over five years, and if today we have been able to produce a constitutional instrument of which we may be justly proud, a tribute is due to that band of able and patriotic men of whom the most notable was the late Dr. Tej Bahadur Sapru, who, in the face of great difficulties, hammered out the principles and laid down the foundations of our new political structure.

This Constitution is a formidable document of nearly 400 clauses and many schedules. But divested of details its main features are easily understood. I venture to invite your attention to some of them as we ourselves and, I fervently hope, our children and children's children for generations, will live a life of freedom under the Constitution we have given to ourselves.

The most outstanding feature of the new Constitution is of course its democratic character. Political power is vested in the people, in the most extensive sense of that word, and every institution derives its authority from the people and is responsible to the people. The democracy that it has enfranchised is easily the largest in the world: of India's 360 million people, no less than 170 million are entitled to vote. This is a figure which is larger than the total population of the United States and does not fall far short of the population of the Soviet Union. India's electorate forms one-twelfth of the population of the world.

The second feature to which I would invite attention is that it follows the parliamentary tradition of Britain, centralising the power in a national parliament to which the executive is responsible for all its actions. The laws and conventions under which the parliamentary democracy of England has been functioning constitute the assumptions on which our government is based. An uninstructed foreigner reading our Constitution cannot fail to gain the impression that the Head of the State is all-powerful. Under the letter of the law everything is left to him, and he is merely advised by a Council of Ministers. Nowhere is it provided that the Head of the State should follow that advice or that the Cabinet itself is strictly accountable to the legislature for its actions. This may appear at first sight to be a weakness, but essentially it is an affirmation of our faith in the maintenance of political freedom by methods which have been tested by two centuries of experience in Europe.

The centralised authority of Parliament is indeed a far cry from the vague demands for a political structure based on rural autonomy which was claimed to be in conformity with India's genius. The overwhelming requirements of national security, no less than the urgently felt need for a planned renovation of society, has compelled us to repudiate in the most explicit manner any scheme which gave to the Central Government only limited powers, and the result has been the creation of a political structure, perhaps more centralised than any that India had in the past, for even under the British rulers one-third of India had remained outside their legislative and administrative competence.

The third and no less important feature of our Constitution is the provision of what are known as Fundamental Rights. The mere incorporation into the Constitution of such clauses as those providing for the abolition of untouchability, for the equality of men and women, in a country where contrary practices had for long claimed the sanction of immemorial usage, if not of religion, is itself important; but the provision for the enforcement of these rights through processes of law adds to their significance, as it is also the clearest evidence of what I consider to be the basic factor of our democratic life, the Supremacy of Law.

Now, it is obvious that these great principles enshrined in our Constitution, the nation-state, which does not recognise divisions of caste, creed and race, democracy and fundamental rights, on which our life is to be based, are not derived from the traditions of India's past. The idea of a nation-state in which all parts of the country shared the power and participated in the government, in which everyone felt, thought and acted as an Indian, is of recent growth in India and cannot be traced back either to the Vedas or to later Hindu writings.

Nor can democracy in the sense we understand it today be reconciled with the social thought of the Hindus, which was essentially non-egalitarian, believing in a hierarchic and unchanging division of society into castes, with differing rights. So far as fundamental rights are concerned, it would not be unfair to hold that their provision in the Constitution was necessitated as much by the determination of the liberal Hindus to consolidate and safeguard the gains which they had secured in their struggles against orthodoxy during the past hundred years, as by the fear of the minority groups about their cultural, religious and political rights. The reformation of Hinduism under the impact of the West had gained for the Hindu masses the right of legal and social equality, had raised the status of women, had given to the untouchables equality, social freedom and political rights. What the Constitution does by laying these down as fundamental rights is to ensure that these gains of a hundred years of social activity are not overwhelmed and destroyed by any revival of obscurantism, by any desire to go back to the doctrines of the past.

Clearly, our new democratic, egalitarian and secular state is not built upon the foundations of ancient India, or of Hindu thought. What we have created is something new, as the life we hope to live and the civilisation we strive to develop are also something new. Where do, then, the origins of our new India lie? They have their roots in the common tradition that civilised humanity has developed during the last one hundred and fifty years, as a result of activities everywhere but primarily in Europe. It is meaningless to hold that the tradition of democracy and equality is European. We are equally the inheritors of it, in the sense that the valid thought and experience of every country is the inheritance of all. There is neither copyright nor patent in political ideas, and if the doctrine of political equality was first tried in France, it became, from the moment of its trial, the property of the whole world. In the same way, if parliamentary democracy was tried and perfected in England, it does not, by virtue of that fact, become a special quality of England or a monopoly of the English people. The conception of economic justice, the extension of the content of liberty to include equitable distribution of wealth, may be socialist in origin, but it is no longer the monopoly of socialist thinking.

Nor is it a fact that India is merely borrowing these ideas, as one borrows the fashions of others. A little consideration would show that India was an active participant and therefore a direct inheritor of the revolutionary ideas of the 19th century. Condorcet was still writing when Ram Mohan Roy was thinking out for himself a new basis for Hindu society. The Revolutionary Club of Seringapatam with Citizen Tipu as a member may sound fantastic, but it is clear evidence that the doctrines of the French Revolution permeated into India even at that time. A banquet in the Calcutta Town Hall to celebrate the Spanish Revolution of 1823 may have been no more than a futile gesture, but it serves to emphasise how India had even then felt her solidarity with democratic movements. Very few people realise that from the beginning of the 19th century, Indian thought, feeling and experience have been closely connected with developments in Europe, and this movement, of which the outstanding champions were men like Maharshi Dwijendranath Tagore, Keshab Chandra Sen, and the fathers of the National Congress, represented not the imitative capacity of the Indian mind but the genuine reflection of a world-wide intellectual process. Looked at from this point of view, the doctrines on which our New India has been built cannot be considered as foreign merely because they are not derived from the sacred books of the Hindus, or do not conform to the social theories or political practices of ancient empires. We are in fact the inheritors of the traditions of both India and of the world, and we can legitimately claim as our own what we have assimilated from other countries.

Truly, what modern India represents is a new civilisation, a synthesis between the East and the West. The history of India, in all its great ages, has shown that as a people we have never been exclusive in our attitude towards other countries and have freely assimilated what other nations had to contribute. Indian civilisation has in the past been like an ever-broadening river into which has flown the waters of many streams, giving to it depth, width and volume, but maintaining its own individual characteristics. It is therefore rather a matter of pride to us than of shame that as a result of a hundred and fifty years of association with Britain we have been able to effect a synthesis of the East and the West, a synthesis which has expressed itself in every sphere of national life, in our social relationships, in our conceptions of law, in our literature, art and other expressions of æsthetic activity, and in our political institutions. While remaining Indians and holding fast to those traditions of the past which our experience shows us to be valid, we have been able to create at least the beginnings of a new life.

The part that the English language has played in this revolution is one to which I should like to draw attention. It is our education in the English language during a period of over a hundred years that has enabled us to share equally with the peoples of Europe the garnered harvest of world enlightenment. It should not be understood that I am advocating the continuance of English as the national language of India. India must have her own national language, not only because our self-respect as an independent nation requires it, but because we know from experience that the creative activity of the Indian mind cannot find adequate expression through a foreign language. Though India must therefore cherish her own national language, and must concentrate her efforts in developing it as a medium fit for the expression of our highest thoughts, I think it will be a great mistake on that account to deny the advantages or belittle the importance of English in New India. It is no longer a question of accepting the language of our alien rulers. English has ceased to be a national language in the sense that it is the language of a single people. Like Arabic, Spanish, French and Russian, it is the language of a civilisation, as Sanskrit was at an earlier age, when inscriptions in such far off countries as Kambuja, Champa and Java were composed in Sanskrit. No doubt our own national language will one day reach that position and be the international medium of a new civilisation.

But today even its national character remains only an aspiration.

If English is the language of the new culture with which we have been associated, it is imperative that till our national language is able to assume that position we should continue to cultivate English assiduously, not because it is a language which gives us contact with the outside world, but because its continued cultivation is necessary for our own intellectual growth. The spirit of intolerance which tries to deceive our youth by claiming to be nationalist would like to see the cry of Quit India extended to the English language and whatever else smacks of European culture. The evil spirit of intellectual obscurantism donning the robes of orthodoxy and appealing to doubtful texts in ancient books would like to cut at the roots of our freedom of thinking by attacking the English language. And others there are who think that their love of their own language is best expressed by asking for the exclusion of English. These and other similar forces which are seeking to anathemise English in the name of patriotism, orthodoxy and love of the mother tongue are trying to take us back to an age of Chaturvarnya and Varanashrama Dharma which they falsely and ignorantly identify with Hindu culture.

And what indeed is the Hindu culture about which these men speak so loudly and so vehemently? I venture to think that true culture, while it may have regional characteristics, arising from racial traditions, can only be universal. The Indian people have made valuable contributions to the culture of the world. But we should not forget that it is only a segment of the culture of the world, only a partial and imperfect expression of the human spirit. No nation can progress and take its place in the world by living within itself and claiming that its people are the chosen of God and all that is of value is to be found in their country. The great Muslim scholar, Al Beruni, who visited India in the 11th century, noticed this tendency among the Hindus of his day, and if during the last one hundred years we have made notable progress, it is because the Hindu leaders of the time realised that India could regain her place among progressive nations only if she was prepared to share in the intellectual, social and political achievements of other countries. The great Hindu Reformation, which in its extent, massiveness and far-reaching consequences is a movement comparable to the great intellectual revolutions of Europe, but about which so little has ben written and so little known outside, was the outcome of this realisation that Hindu culture, whatever its greatness and whatever its value, will survive only if it assimilates the experience of other cultures, and renovates itself by abandoning what has become old and meaningless, and re-interprets whatever remains in terms of modern life. The danger today is that we, in the intoxication of our new-found freedom, are showing marked tendencies of desiring to forget this fundamental truth. Indian civilisation has to be and will be preserved. It will grow with added vigour and greater vitality; but it will grow and attain greatness only *if we hold fast to the doctrines of our renaissance, that national* cutures are not exclusive, and are in fact the result of continuous assimilation with one's own experience the experience of other peoples all over the world. The tendency to withdraw unto ourselves and to proclaim the greatness of our culture as being unique, based on some special gifts which other nations do not share, can to my mind lead only to disaster.

What are these special qualities of the Indian mind about which one often hears? The most widely claimed quality is what is known as "spirituality". It is quite often claimed that the West is materialist and the East is spiritual. This view, which one often comes across, will on examination be found to be utterly meaningless. What spirituality can we claim when we denied elementary human rights to a great section of our own people; when we permitted in the name of religion practices which revolted the conscience of the world such as the dedication of Devadasis to temples? What kind of spirituality is it that does not help to develop a social conscience, which neglects the poor and the orphaned, which remains unmoved in the face of calamities like plague and famine which affect millions? The highest form of spirituality is that which helps man to develop a social conscience, or in the words of Gita, to dedicate one's acts to *Loka Sangraha* or the welfare of the world. This idea of claiming special virtues for the Indian mind was but an aspect of escapism, a facile method by which in the days of our political degradation and dependence we upheld our self-respect. We felt that by claiming an imponderable virtue for us we could deceive ourselves about our real position in the world. Today when we are free and can bravely look others in the face, there is no justification for holding so absurd a view. Till we shed the feeling that we are not like others, that we have special merits and special qualities, that we are spiritual and our culture is superior, there is no possibility for India to advance.

In a few days time [1950] India will become a sovereign independent republic, associated freely and voluntarily with a great community of nations. The change from a Dominion to a Republic may seem to be only a matter of form, as we have been an independent country for over two years now. But it has a deep significance which we should not forget. It is, I consider, a solemn declaration of our break with past traditions, of our determination to start on a new life, of our acceptance of our responsibilities as a full-grown member of the family of nations. It is an affirmation of our ideas of not standing for privileges, our faith in the equality of man, of our conviction that humanity can march to its goal only through co-operative effort. These are the responsibilities that the new Republican India places on the shoulders of the youth of today. This is what you young men who are now receiving your education, or completing it by receiving your degrees, inherit from your elders. Your success or failure in life will be judged not by the positions you will occupy in the future or the money you will leave to your children, but by the extent you have, by your individual and collective effort, furthered these ideas and handed them down with extended meaning and enriched experience to your successors.

To the graduates who receive their degrees today, I have only a few words to say. You are now about to leave these cloistered halls after the completion of your academic education. You have received at the hands of your Vice-

Chancellor the degrees and diplomas to which you are entitled as a result of many years of hard work and training. You will now go out to face the world with the responsibilities that education throws on you, for I have no doubt that the time and money which you have spent and the labour you have put in have been wholly wasted unless they have taught you that education confers on you not merely new opportunities and openings but responsibilities towards society. The difference between an educated man and an uneducated one lies not so much in the knowledge that one has accumulated through books, but in the social conscience which one develops, the discipline one acquires, the values one cultivates, and above all, the spirit of charity and toleration which one develops.

It would be trite to say that the world is going through a moral crisis for which there is no parallel in history. It provides a challenge to every one's spiritual integrity, for the present division of the world into hostile camps, professing mutually destructive ideologies but believing in exclusive truth, requires of each one to make up his mind in regard to problems of fundamental importance. There was never a period in history when people did not believe that they were living in exceptional times, that the world was changing for the worse. But no one can deny that the situation today represents much more than a crisis. The world is facing a dissolution of the ideas which had been held as axiomatic over a considerable period of time, a breakdown of institutions which had by long familiarity been considered as a part of natural order, a denial of values which had long been accepted as absolute: in fact all the signs of the change of an epoch Over vast areas of the world men are struggling towards the establishment of an order of society which it is accepted is incompatible with what exists in the rest of the world. And this struggle has penetrated into every sphere of life, literature, art and sciences, no less than politics, economics, and social relationships. It has become a personal problem for each one, for no man who claims to be educated can avoid taking a decision on the moral issues posed before the world.

Each one of you who goes out to face the world and its problems today, equipped, I would fain believe, with the necessary standards of judgement, will have to take a decision on this question, for it is one to which you cannot remain indifferent. Not only your own individual future, but the future of our country will depend on the nature of the decision that the young men of today take on the fundamental conflict of morality which faces mankind today.

Whatever the decision we individually arrive at there can be no question that India will have to build up a new life. That new life is not only a question of economic betterment, though it is undoubtedly an important aspect of it. It is not merely the development and successful working of new political institutions; though that also is important. It is much more than the building up of national strength in a material sense, though that also is necessary, if we are to survive as a great nation. The challenge that the demand for a New Life presents to each one of you is the creation of a new set of values, applicable alike to the individual and to the community, which harmonises the conception of individual freedom with discipline, charity and tolerance with firm convictions and, above all, a social consciousness which realises that material wealth is for the service of the community.

In the creation of this New Life we will perforce have to give up much of what our forefathers held to be sacred, and which by a curious process has come to be identified with India itself. Does anyone believe that a new life in India can develop and the ideas which have transformed society elsewhere permeate the masses if we hold fast to encrusted tradition, and hug with affection every relic of the past as being part of Indian culture? We have to examine each one of our institutions in terms not only of its utility today but of its conformity with the ideals of justice, equality and liberty, which we have laid down solemnly as the basic principles of our new life. Social tradition which custom represents is no doubt of value, as it ensures continuinty, the carry-over of national individuality, but where such custom, as in the case of caste relationships, disabilities enforced against groups, subordination of women, operate against national life, or as in other cases go against our economic well-being, they have to be ruthlessly rooted out. This is the great fight in which each one of you has to be a soldier throughout your life, for compromise on such issues now involves danger to the nation, to the future we are looking forward to as a progressive people, carrying forward the life of humanity.

The responsibilities of the youth of an independent country are indeed great, for the duty of not only maintaining but enlarging national freedom falls on its shoulders. We would fail as a nation and disappoint the hopes which the fathers of our independence cherished if the young men and women who come out of the universities today do not realise the immensity of the trust that they are taking over. It is one of the pitfalls unavoidable in the case of a country which has newly achieved independence to glory in its greatness, to feel, and express a sense of national egoism, to give less consideration than is due to the claims of others. Nothing in my opinion is more dangerous to a young nation. I would venture to emphasise this point, for we are doubly prone to it. We often tend to equate our size, population and resources with national greatness, and equally what we believe to be our past glory as an assurance of our present position. Do not let us forget that our greatness is only potential and whether it becomes a reality depends on the way the challenge of the New Life is faced by our youth.

The New Dynamism

I CONSIDER it a great privilege to have been invited to address the Convocation of this University. Standing on this hallowed ground, where the Nalanda University once flourished, it is but natural that one should feel not only a deep sense of humility in the presence of so much of tradition and history but also a pride in the continuity of our life and of our ideals. It is natural for us to feel that pride, for Nalanda was nothing provincial; it was truly national and catholic in character and international in outlook. The succession of eminent teachers who came from different parts of India and presided over the University bore witness to its national and catholic character. Dharmapala, the Head Abbot at the beginning of the 7th century, was a Tamil nobleman from Conjeevaram in the south; Jinamitra, another renowned teacher, came from the Andhra country; Silabhadra, the saintly teacher of Yuan Chwang, was a converted Brahmin from the eastern area, probably from Pragjotisha. What better evidence is needed to establish the truly national character of Nalanda?

That its outlook was international is equally borne out by records. A Srivijaya monarch, from what is now the Republic of Indonesia, endowed one of the institutions of the University. Under a "tooth brush tree" in its grounds the Korean monk, Huih Nieh, whose Sanskritised name was Aryavarman, sat and copied sacred manuscripts. The great Master of the Law, Yuan Chwang, travelled from distant Chang An to sit at the

Convocation Address at the Patna University, 1954.

feet of its illustrious teachers. From its sacred precincts scholars travelled far and wide, to Tibet, to Ceylon, to Java and the Far-Eastern countries. From the neighbouring University of Vikramasila went forth monks and teachers who transformed the spiritual life of Tibet.

If I mention these facts it is only to emphasise to the youth of Bihar the tradition of internationalism to which they are heirs. In the days when Magadha stood in the vanguard of thought there was no narrowness of spirit, no idea of provincialism, but a wide and generous feeling of humanity, a desire to acquire and to spread knowledge, a desire to serve humanity. It is that outlook in the youth of a country that makes a free people great.

In an independent society the first requirement is intellectual curiosity. The virtues and qualities which were required when the country was under foreign rule had, of necessity, to be different from those which we have to cherish when the nation is free and independent. The youth of the generation that struggled and won national freedom had as their motivating force the desire for liberation. Today the motivation has naturally to be different. The new generation has to think of consolidating, broadening and giving new content to the freedom that we have won. This requires a new approach to life, a different emphasis, almost different social virtues and ambitions.

A free society can only live and grow on intellectual curiosity, for in the absence of that curiosity it will fall back in the race and will in due course lose its freedom. No country or people can live on borrowed thought or second-hand science. It is true that knowledge, science and thought do not belong to any particular country and there is no grosser error than to talk of Western science, or Eastern mathematics, for knowledge, once discovered, becomes the property of the human race. Since knowledge, science and thought are the inheritance of the civilised man, their progress can only be through common effort and, unless we contribute our share, we shall always be behind others, not only in the realm of knowledge itself but in the realm of material progress. In the history of human advancement there is nothing which is better established and capable of clearer proof than the fact that material progress is dependent on advancing knowledge. India is only slowly awakening to this fact for until quite recently we were content to build on the knowledge that others had gained and transmitted to us. We were in fact living on the charity of others: but trying at the same time to save our self-respect by loudly proclaiming the glories of our past, the contributions which ancient India had made to the progress of science. No one denies these contributions and their importance to the history of civilisation. India was indeed a free and progressive country in the days when she made those contributions for which she is still remembered but when the lamp of learning began to burn dim our freedom also vanished and our greatness became a memory. Our life in the family of free nations will be no more than of poor relations unless through our own efforts we contribute to that freedom of mind which is the outcome of intellectual curiosity.

The first call to the youth of today, indeed their first duty, is, therefore, to promote knowledge. Unfortunately in India, the traditional desire of young men is for service. I do not by any means deprecate those who spell out their future in terms of appointments, promotions, transfers and finally honourable retirement with the reward of a substantial pension. There will always be, in all societies, men who prefer safety to adventure, security to the risk of failure, appearance of authority, however unreal, to the substance of achievement. Service, administration and office are for such people. They form indeed a worthy and useful class. We must have public servants just as we must have shopkeepers, businessmen and all other organised agencies for carrying on the life of the nation. But let us not forget that administration, however efficient, and service, however well paid, secure and glamorous, represent the static side of life. The administrator is always on the side of what exists and generally serves the cause of what is decaying. A very distinguished thinker once observed that law represents the progressive thought of the day before yesterday and clearly the administrator who bases himself on law and whose thoughts are shaped and actions controlled by laws, rules and regulations cannot therefore be accused of a desire for progress.

Young men still hanker after government service for two reasons: first the prestige that superior services under the government gave and still retain as a kind of sunset glow; and secondly because of the sense of financial security it provided. Let me assure you the first is a vanishing factor. The second is not one to which youth should attach undue weight. It is true that by becoming a scientist or a creative worker in any field you will not ensure your financial security. But it is well that this generation of free India should remember that if their elders who fought for the nation's freedom had thought in terms of financial security we should not now be living as free men.

If the best among the youth of a nation prefer the sheltered lives of government servants and their ambitions are limited by the prospects of service then that nation must inevitably decay.

No foreign government could afford to encourage a spirit of adventure in a subject people. With independence the position is different. We now recognise that young men who persevere in their attempts to scale the Himalayan peaks, scientists who plan to explore the deeps, pioneers who sacrifice themselves in testing planes and establishing speed records, creative artists who give form to new ideas and others who cultivate the sense of mental and physical adventure are the people on whom the hope of the country for progress and advancement rests. Those others maintain and preserve the framework within which society lives. But to the growth of the nation they contribute but little. So I venture to appeal to those of you who have a spirit of intellectual adventure to choose for yourselves work which ranges you on the side of progress, where the mind is free to think and where you can contribute something to the world of ideas or of achievement.

Free India faces many problems, some inherited from our history, others arising from the special circumstances of the present day. Among those which we have inherited from our past is the incipient rivalry, if not conflict, between national and regional cultures which has expressed itself on what has been rather crudely christened as linguism. As this is one of the major issues which agitate the thinking mind of India today, I may be permitted to offer a few observations about it here.

When Indian culture witnessed its present revival, from the utter decadence into which it had fallen over most areas of India in the 18th century, it was based on three new factors—a revived religion, a linguistic vehicle whose reach extended to every corner of India, and the formation of new classes of society, drawn from many sections, capable of transmitting new ideas to the community as a whole. The revival of religion which started with Ram Mohan Roy was no doubt a movement within the fold of Hinduism, but it is well to emphasise that the basic culture of India being based on Hindu traditions, the revival was truly national and not sectional. The second factor which made it possible was the growth of a national language, national in the sense that its sway extended to the whole country. The phenomenal growth of our regional languages during this period would have made the growth of a national Indian culture impossible without the advantage of a dominant language. That was provided for over a hundred years by English. It is necessary to remember that much of the literature of our religious revival from Ram Mohan to Aurobindo is in English and Ramakrishna's own message spread to all parts of India through the effective use of English by Vivekananda and his successors. Today English is in the process of being displaced by Hindi as the national language of India. That is undoubtedly as it should be, but it has revealed an inherent danger against which we have to guard. The richness of India's regional languages, the great wealth of thought and beauty which they enshrine, is something of which the people who use those languages are naturally proud. The rich and diversified culture of India finds its best expression in those languages. We can only neglect them at our peril, for those regional cultures, derived as they are from a common inheritance, contribute richly to the common culture. In our desire for unity, in our emphasis on our common nationhood, in the pride of our common culture, we should not forget the importance of these great languages and the culture they represent. But—and this is the danger—our national culture will surely disintegrate and with it our political freedom, if the basic unity of our life becomes blurred by the growth of too powerful a regionalism. It is only when there is a dominant national culture that regional variations can contribute to it. Otherwise the local variations will themselves become small stagnant pools deprived of the currents and tides of the greater whole. The danger in India today is the tendency on the part of regional cultures to usurp the position of national culture in their own areas, arising mainly from the virility and hold of the great local languages. The fact that until now it was English that was performing the functions of a national language and a loyalty to that language was impossible has helped in the growth of these tendencies towards disintegration. It seems therefore vitally important that within the next few years we should develop our national language as a medium of all-India thought and culture and not permit the present tendency to over-emphasise the importance of local cultures to undermine the unity of our life.

It is not unusual in India for groups to be formed for the revival or promotion of languages which at one time had significance but which, with the greater integration of major languages, have ceased to be of importance. For instance, there is a Rajasthani institute at Bikaner which is doing considerable work on that language. Maithili again is a language with a great past and I have heard of associations for the promotion of Garwali and Dogri. All these linguistic groups are, let it be remembered, in what is known as Hindi-speaking areas, regions where Hindi has become the dominant language of culture. While I have no doubt that research in these local languages and their revival as a matter of scholarly interest will help to enrich Hindi and add content to our national culture, any attempt to revive them as media of present-day life can only strengthen the process of disintegration.

As one who has devoted a considerable portion of his life to the cultivation of the mother tongue I am sure I will not be accused of under-estimating the value of our regional languages or the necessity of basing our local cultures on them. But in India, where the sentiment of national unity was revived and strengthened slowly through the domination of English, we will most surely be trying to nullify that achievement if the national language by which we desire to replace it does not acquire a truly national character and reflect that spirit of unity and sentiment which forms the basis of our nationhood.

One significant development of linguistic nationalism which has caused much heart searching has been the demand voiced in many quarters for state units based on languages. You will not expect me to discuss that question here. But from what I have stated previously you will, I am sure, realise its importance to our future as a nation.

India in the past had two focii of culture, of civilisation, one south of the Vindhyas and the other in the Gangetic valley, both mutually interacting and influencing and creating our common national life. Our distinguished and scholarly President, Dr. Rajendra Prasad, once remarked that while all the avatars were in North India, all the acharyas came from the south. It is the combination of avatars and acharyas that makes our life. It is the blending of the north and the south, of Aryavarta and Dakshinapatha, that makes Bharatavarsha. The existence of these two focii, the two generating sources of culture, is necessary for the natural growth of our life. Any attempt by the one part to dominate over the other politically, economically, or culturally will only end in disaster. The defeat of Harsha by Pulikesan, the failure of Aurangzeb in the Deccan, the disaster which the Maratha armies met at Panipat—all tell the same tale. The vigour, persistence and continuity of Dravidian culture in the south, in spite of the acceptance of Sanskrit and the dominance of the tradition which is embodied in the classics of that language, demonstrate on the other hand that a genuine harmony could be established if the integrity and independence of the southern focus of India's life are adequately recognised. It is fortunate for India that our leaders during the last hundred years fully recognised and emphasised this fact. It is equally a happy augury for the future that those who shape our destiny today are alive to this fundamental fact of our history.

What is necessary in India today perhaps more than anything else is a proper appreciation of India's history. It is a most deplorable fact that during the last hundred years, when the history of India came to be systematically studied, the emphasis had, of necessity, to be laid not on the growth of the Indian people, but on the political activities of our alien rulers. So the substance of history, the transformation of Hindu Society during the last 150 years, the reformation of Hindu Religion—an event of far-reaching consequence comparable both in its quality and its magnitude to the counter-reformation of the Catholic Church—the growth of new classes, the changes in economic structure, and the development of national sentiment, in short, the history of the Indian people, was neglected in favour of the wars and campaigns of the East India Company and the activities of insignificant noblemen who succeeded one after another to the *gadi* of Fort William. One result of this emphasis on the political annals of British India was that our more self-respecting historians devoted themselves to earlier periods, bringing to light forgotten dynasties, empires and kingdoms, laboriously building up through the study of inscriptions, coins and literary texts a continuous story as the foundation of our national pride. The history of the Mauryas, the Bhara Sivas, the Vakatakas, the Guptas and other great imperial dynasties is undoubtedly important, not only because India's life is unbroken and continuous, but because our own traditions would become dead and foreign to us unless we have a proper appreciation of their growth. But however much we may take pride in the achievements of the earlier periods, it is the immediate past that lives with us. It is the history of the last two hundred years that weighs heaviest on us.

Life as we live it today is the result of the activity of the Indian people during the British rule, their reactions to the challenge of foreign domination, the adjustments and compromises which resulted from the confrontation of a powerful but alien way of life, their acceptance of the new learning which came from the West. In fact it would not be incorrect to say that our mental conditioning today is the result predominently of the last two hundred years of our history. To see that period of our history in proper perspective, uninfluenced both by the prejudices of nationalism and by the propaganda of imperialism, is one of the first duties of this generation in India.

Surely, not only of India, but of all Asia, for we know that, today as in the past, the fate of the Asian countries is bound together inextricably. We know a great deal of European history, not only the history of England, but of France, Germany and Italy. But we know nothing of the history of Persia or China, our two great neighbours. With Persia our relations had been intimate from the beginning of history till the establishment of British rule. With China for over 1500 years we maintained close contacts. In the immediately preceding age of the history of our three countries, though we knew but little of each other, our fates were again intertwined. It is, as we now know, the establishment of British authority in India that led to Western interference in Persia's affairs. Even more significantly, it was British power in India which enabled European nations to dominate China for a hundred years. Today the nations of Asia know this and it is for that reason that I would venture to appeal to University authorities in India to make Asian history an important subject of study.

We hear a great deal of talk about our civilisation. It is no doubt ancient, abiding and impressive. But there is an undeniable tendency to equate it with the monuments of the past, with the achievements of our ancestors. But I would like to emphasise that it is not the glories of Nalanda, the mural paintings of Ajanta, or the haunting beauty of the Taj Mahal or even the great literary works or the philosophical systems of the past that exclusively constitute our civilisation. They are indeed matters in which we can and should take legitimate pride, but the new civilisation that is developing around us, the new vision of India which is rising before us, should also move us to enthusiasm. Not far from here is the great Damodar Valley Project, with its numerous dams, with its power stations, with its large lakes and navigable canals. All over India today there are growing up many such constructions, vast schemes meant to better the life of our people. These are not always beautiful from the aesthetic point of view like the Kailas Temple at Ellora or the Taj Mahal at Agra. But they are also the creations of our brains and the work of our hands and who will say that they do not add to beauty when they enable us to transform parched deserts into flowering gardens, to tame dangerous rivers and control their destructive floods and, more than all, feed hungry millions and give them happiness? Civilisation is not mere material prosperity, but material prosperity is essential for all civilisation. In India itself it was only during periods when India was materially prosperous that her civilisation advanced and we created things of notable beauty. One has only to read the classical literature of Sanskrit to know that the society reflected there was one of luxury and prosperity. So, let those who moan that free India is not building new temples which vie with Ellora, or constructing monuments which equal the Taj, remember that the transformation of life that is being attempted today, not merely in our irrigation schemes, in our new factories, but in the villages themselves, is creating a higher and greater civilisation than we have ever enjoyed, a culture not confined to classes and groups but extending to the entire nation. That is the civilisation to the building of which each one of you can contribute; that is the civilisation of which we can be legitimately proud, because not only have we inherited it but have helped to create it.

The situation in the world today could not fail to appear confused to the most careful observer. Whichever side you turn, you will find that old loyalties have disappeared, that principles and ideas which had been considered axiomatic are now no longer accepted, that the differences between nations are based on different ideas of life and politics and, more than all, the world is in the grip of a grim and fearsome uncertainty not only in regard to values, but in regard to its future itself. All these are the characteristics one finds when human society moves from one era into another; when a period of history which had a certain unity in thought, ideals and human and international relationships is in the process of being replaced by another. The ancient Hindus described it as the change of a *Yuga*. That is the process we are now going through. It is not an unusual experience in history. The period of transition from one age to another is always one of uncertainty, social maladjustment and economic disturbances, the result to a large extent of the disappearance or the eclipse of old empires which had all the appearance of stability and power in the past, of the rise of new states, edging their way on to the international stage, the discredit into which old ideas, which had governed the actions of generations, suddenly fall with the failure of the institutions which they represented or in which they were embodied. In vast areas of Asia and Africa this process may be seen clearly. New Asian states which had not existed or when they existed, as in China, were weak and ineffective, have become major factors in international life. The Western nations are slowly awakening to this fact and a great deal of the political troubles in the East can be traced to the difficulty which the great nations of the past have in adjusting their minds to the changed position. Even where they intellectually accept it, they find it hard to bring about the necessary change in their actions.

How past loyalties and institutions which everyone had accepted as part of the normal life have vanished or broken down may be easily seen by looking around us in India itself. The great princely states of India, which for centuries had been accepted as a part of our life and around which considerable loyalties had grown up, have today become memories of the past. Overnight the structure of princely rule vanished in India. That was only symptomatic of the change that had already come over the country, undermining the influence of the traditional conceptions of life, of *Varnashrama Dharma*, of caste and untouchability, of authority based on social status etc. The great question today is to define the new conceptions which should take the place of those that we have discarded and to give them the binding character and motivating force which are necessary for the working of our new society. Vaguely we realise that these conceptions should be based on democracy, on the right of individuals to freedom of mind and action. It is the work of the new generation to define these things more precisely and to build up our new society on firm foundations.

In a democracy this work of defining and enforcing loyalties can only be the result of the development of a collective conscience. In other forms of society these standards and values are established either by tradition or by authority, and are upheld by the sanctions of religion, of social institutions like monarchy, or by the discipline of a party to which complete submission is postulated as part of a political system. It is the essence of democracy that such loyalty must be voluntary, must be felt and accepted by the great majority as being for the good of both the individual and the community. Democracy has no other ultimate sanction, for to coerce those who deny the moral validity of the principles it stands for or the loyalties it seeks to gain would be the very denial of democracy. This is also the danger to which democracy is exposed. Systems which deny democratic values and reject the loyalties on which the system of democracy is based must continue to have an equal right to persuade the people. It is no argument to say that we cannot tolerate in a democratic society those who deny the basic postulates of democracy. That will be denying our faith. To survive the assaults of other systems, the democratic ideal must become a part of the life of the people, something which they cherish and are prepared to uphold by every kind of sacrifice.

There is one danger to which democracies are strangely susceptible—more especially if, having newly acquired democratic freedom, they develop along with it a fanaticism about their heritage. This is the tendency on the part of democracies to exploit fear; to raise bogeys and create a panicky sense of danger in the minds of the ignorant. This is nothing new in history. Guy Fawkes and Titus Oates are the ignominous ancestors of those who today cry "Religion in danger", and pretend to see spies at every corner. This danger has become immensely greater than in all past ages because the machinery now available for creating mass opinion—cinema, radio and television, not to speak of mass circulation papers catering to the lowest instincts of their readers. The exploitation of fear, whether it is of an imagined enemy across the border or of traitors and spies within the fold, or the supposed indifference of those in authority to the protection of sacred animals, or their neglect of religious duties, is the gravest danger to democracy today. It leads to inquisitions, ostracisms and intolerance in general—the perpetual enemies of democratic freedom. It is only by each one of us contributing to the definition and enforcement of democratic loyalties, the greatest of which is toleration based on freedom, that we can hope to live as a free people.

We are still laying the foundations of our life. To make them solid and firm we must know the strength of our tradition, the true course of our national evolution, not as others have taught us but as we ourselves understand it. More than that, we have to learn from others, and assimilate what we learn and make it a part of ourselves. No country grows to its full stature by depending on itself and there is nothing more likely to cause the downfall of a nation than the strange doctrine which a perverted nationalism proclaims of everything in one's own country being the best in the world. Knowledge, science, skills and organisation on which a nation's greatness depends are not exclusively developed in one country. They have to be accepted from everywhere So in your dedication to the service of the country let not a sense of exclusive pride come into you, for that is the way to downfall.

India is beset with many grave problems. To the youth of today they should act as a challenge, as something which calls forth all their intellectual and physical energies and resources.

It is one of the great lessons of history that it is only by having to face great difficulties that a nation's highest qualities are brought into play. So today we can face the future with optimism for this beloved motherland of ours is opening a new chapter in the history of her greatness.

Regionalism

I AM INDEED happy to have been afforded this opportunity of addressing the Convocation of the Utkal University. Though it is my first visit to Orissa, I have none of the feeling of being a stranger among you for the unique greatness of our country is that though our languages may be different and our climates may vary, we, as inheritors of a common tradition, feel at home everywhere in India. I feel, as others who come to Orissa no doubt feel, that they share with you the sacredness of Puri, the artistic heritage of Bhuvaneshwar and Konarak and other magnificent temples, and, if I may add, feel with you equal pride in the great aspiration now taking shape in the Hirakud Project. A new Utkal is being born, springing not only from the adventurous spirit of the Kalingas of the past who roamed the seas and carried the message of Indian culture far and wide, and from the imagination and skill of the great builders of temples which are still the marvels of the world, but also from the vision of a new India, and the ambition to create a new and better life for her people.

You in Orissa are justly proud of the achievements of your ancestors, of the great kings from Kharavela to the Gajapatis, who have contributed so much to India's culture. I am the last to decry local patriotism and an honourable pride in the greatness of our ancestors, but all over India I have noted with regret a deplorable tendency to create, from the vagueness of our past history, political myths of each being the

Address to the Utkal University Convocation, 1954.

chosen people in India, with unrivalled traditions and outstanding achievements. In a country like ours, with a history extending to over five thousand years, it would indeed be remarkable if there were not periods when each area contributed something of great value, but that should not lead us to the false notion that any particular area in India, whether it be Magadha or Maharashtra, Orissa or Andhra, Tamilnad or Karnataka, can claim that its history outshines that of other areas. Magadha boasts of empires and traces its glory to Jarasandha and a long line of famous monarchs. The Indo-Gangetic Plain, with its great cities of Indraprastha, Hastinapur, Kanauj, Ayodhya and Kosambi, not to speak of the more recent glories of Delhi and Agra, claims even a more assured pre-eminence. The Andhras, who connect themselves with every known dynasty and empire from the time of the Satavahanas to Vijayanagar; the Maharashtra country, which apart from its greatness in the modern period claims equally to be the inheritor of the Rastrakutas, the Chalukyas and the Yadavas, and so on—every part of India affirms and believes in its own special greatness. Indeed each area has contributed greatly to India's life but let me emphasise that regional vanity should not lead us to believe that the gifts of brain and heart, artistic sensibility and military valour are distributed to India in a manifestly unequal manner. With our new-born sense of regional pride we are inclined rather uncritically to see special virtues and claim special gifts for our own areas. This is a grave danger, for one has only to travel to the different parts of India to see how each area has contributed to the unique richness of India's tradition.

The essential point to remember is that no localisation of social, economic or political interest is possible in India today. History in some respects is but the politics of the past and if localisation of today's politics is impossible, localisation of past history will be an utterly reactionary tendency. Take for example your own local history. It is perhaps true as many historians claim that Kapileswara carried the Orissan arms almost to Kanchi. No doubt also a few decades later the great Krishna Deva Raya invaded and conquered portions of Orissa.

What does it mean to us now? Are we to look upon Kapileswara as a great Oriya who had conquered the Andhras, or Krishna Deva Raya as a great Telugu who had humbled the pride of the Oriyas? Such an attitude, I venture to submit, would be contrary to our sense of national unity. We have to look upon both of them as great Indian rulers, who in different ways contributed to the development of our traditions.

The enlargement of the field of political phenomena is the outstanding characteristic of our period. This is a world-wide fact, though of special interest to India. Today, in every aspect of life we are dependent on a wider whole. No state in India, singly, even if it were dreaming of its greatness in a mythical golden age, can undertake a multi-purpose project like that at Hirakud, or contemplate an iron and steel factory like the Hindustan Steel. The cost involved, the technical skills required, the sustained planning and execution which are essential if these plans are to succeed are beyond the resources of a single state. This is true of most of what is being done in India to build up a new society. All our work is interrelated, some more obviously so than others. While it is clear that the economic rebuilding has to be on an all-India basis, has to be planned and carried out with a national vision, it is not equally clear to most people that in such fields as education and public health, which are reserved in our Constitution for the states, an all-India policy has equally become unavoidable. A moment's consideration would show that in the matter of education, for example, a general uniformity of standards, a common agreement about the subjects to be taught and other similar considerations limit effectively the authority of the states.

Let me not be misunderstood as advocating a reversion to a centralised government. Federation is a constitutional device, an administrative arrangement which no one questions or disputes. But the problem is slightly different. It is one of the misfortunes of politics that we generally carry on with institutions even after their *raison d'être* has vanished and try to infuse life into things that are dead merely because we are familiar with them. The sovereignty of the units in a federation is a conception of a similar kind. In the United States of America, where the system was evolved, the thirteen states were originally independent sovereign units and were persuaded to part with some of their sovereignty only with great difficulty—and that also in the face of possible danger to their security. And though the doctrine of state independence is still dear to American politicians, it was no less a person than President Wilson who described the American historical process as one of changing the United States from a plural noun to a singular, from the United States *are* to the United States *is*. In this connection I would like to quote to you a remarkable passage from the Farewell Address of George Washington to the People of the United States. "The unity of Government", said Washington, "which constitutes you one people is also now dear to you. It is justly so; for it is a main pillar in the edifice of your real independence, the support of your tranquillity at home, your peace abroad; of your safety, of your prosperity, of that very liberty which you so highly prize. But as it is easy to foresee that, from different causes and from different quarters, much pains will be taken, many artifices employed, to weaken in your minds the conviction of this truth; as this is the point in your political fortress against which the batteries of internal and external enemies will be most constantly and actively (though often covertly and insidiously) directed, it is of infinite moment that you should estimate the immense value of your national union to your collective and individual happiness; that you should cherish a cordial, habitual and immovable attachment to it (to the Centre) accustoming yourself to think and speak of it as of the Palladium of your political safety and prosperity; watching for its preservation with jealous anxiety; discountenancing whatever may suggest even a suspicion that it can be abandoned; and indignantly growing upon every attempt to alienate any portion of our country from the rest, or to enfeeble the sacred ties which now link together the various parts."

Even at that time, just ten years after the American Constitution was inaugurated, the greatest of American statesmen felt it necessary to warn his countrymen in ringing words that there could be no rivalry between the rights of the centre and of the units, that the national government alone was the palladium of political safety and prosperity, and that every individual and every part were bound to it by sacred ties. If that was so in a country of which the thirteen states were independent before the union, how much more true it is in our case where such independence as the states of the union possess was conferred on them by the Constitution and was in no way inherent in their own history. But though the independence of our states is notional, still the tendency has been noticeable for each unit to consider itself a sovereign state, jealous of its rights, and sensitive about anything which might even distantly affect its powers. In a country like India, with its regional disparities, with its local traditions and languages, the necessity of encouraging policies and programmes that strengthen our unity is so obvious, specially when on that unity are dependent both our political safety and our prosperity. It is unnecessary to argue the point about safety. Washington, in the passage quoted above, had to emphasise that point for there were states in the American Union then which affected to believe that there was no question of the safety of the new state being threatened by anyone. But the question of prosperity is, we have now come to realise, an equally national problem. Prosperity in the modern world depends on three essential things, research work at the highest level in science, the application of the results of research for the better utilisation of national resources, both industrial and agricultural, and a planned economy which takes every aspect of life into consideration. All these can only be undertaken effectively at the national level. It has only to be stated in terms to be accepted by reasonable men, that much as we should cherish our regional life, and devote ourselves wholeheartedly to the work in the state, district and village, it is only by strengthening what Washington called "the sacred ties which link together the various parts", and by looking at our major problems from the national and not from a parochial point of view that we can safeguard our liberties and achieve the prosperity which we so earnestly desire.

The great movement of our time has been everywhere the centralisation of power. This is a movement that has been gradual and has therefore passed practically unnoticed. It has been truly remarked that events that take shape over a period of years will not be found described in state papers or memoirs. The growth of the power of the State is an event of this character. This power of the State, all-pervasive, reaching every nook and corner, affecting all classes, touching all institutions and relationships, is something quite new in the world. But whether the conception be that of a Austinian State claiming the totality of powers as its attribute, or of the dictatorship of the proletariat, the common factor that differentiates the modern state from previous political phenomena is its brazen, unabashed claim to control every aspect of human life. An eminent French writer, Paul Valery, has attempted to define the modern omnipotent state in the following words:

"You can picture to yourself a monarch . . . a man, but a man who can do many things and can control many others. He owns the entire country, in the sense that all other owners possess only by the virtue of the protection he gives them and must pay him tribute. He can enrich, impoverish, elevate and cast people down; exile or put to death whom ever he wishes; build and destroy, make war or make peace, organise, enforce regulations, permit or forbid. He is accountable to nobody . . . . Let us start from this image. Let us work for a moment on this idea of an all-powerful man. Take away all that is human, without reducing his power: suppose him to be exempt from age or death. Time has no hold upon him. That is not all. Take from him all sensitiveness, for this immortal has no need of a heart . . . neither senses nor heart. As for mind . . . indeed I am not too sure what the mind of the state might be."

It is clear that as against this State there is no method of resistance open to the individual. Power becomes administrative in its means and impersonal in its action. The adjustment of the individual to the state in whose presence the mightiest is less than dust and by whose condescension we enjoy whatever rights we are said to possess is a problem of compelling importance for the next generation, more than it is for us of the age that is now passing. It is you, young men and women of today, who have to face this issue, for it is indeed an issue which cannot be shirked.

Human beings have always attached value to liberty. It has always been a motivating force in history. Even in ancient autocracies, where rulers enunciated the doctrine that the monarch was the State or claimed to be the Son of Heaven, or a Naradeva, there were overriding conceptions which limited a monarch's authority. The most powerful of medieval emperors had to go in sack-cloth and ashes in mid-winter to Conossa to confess that there was a power greater than his own and, even in modern times, Bismarck had to learn the same painful lesson. No Son of Heaven could forget the rites and proprieties of Confucian ethics, which were as binding on the Emperor as on his meanest subject. In our own country, no king, however perverse or believing in his own claims to omnipotence, could defy *dharma,* or interfere with society. But the impersonal State of today accepts no *civitas dei,* no *dharma,* no rites and proprieties as binding on itself.

It is because of this almost universal development, no doubt a little less pronounced in our country than elsewhere, that a clear definition of Man's right against the State has become an urgent necessity. The Founding Fathers of our Republic vaguely realised this and incorporated in the Constitution a set of Fundamental Rights. They are undoubtedly important, but unless they represent a coherent theory of political life they would mean but little. The fundamental rights incorporated in our Constitution represent the ideals of liberalism, individual liberty, freedom of speech, freedom of opinion, freedom of religion, etc., the general conceptions of liberty, fraternity and equality. But the tendency of our political life has undeniably been to move away slowly from these liberal conceptions. Would anyone hold that we attach the same importance today to civil liberties as we did some time ago? We have come to examine these abstract rights as they are called in the light of our circumstances today, and the result is that the declaration of fundamental rights is becoming more and more unrelated to the theory and practice of our political life. Of course, it is fully recognised that the content of words like *liberty* and *equality* undergoes change with time. Today liberty is interpreted not merely as the right to be left unmolested in the pursuit of one's normal occupation, but includes the conception of economic liberty, i.e. conditions of life provided by the State under which the individual is not forced to be dependent on others. But the very enlargement of that conception involves restrictions on economic life of a kind which the libertarians of the 19th century did not conceive. Similar results leading to depreciation of the value of human rights follow from other aspects of the enlarged activities of the State, such as national planning, State control of education at all levels, the birth of the bureaucratic state based on large-scale administration, etc. Nearly fifty years ago, a distinguished historian and political observer described these tendencies as leading inevitably to the establishment of the Servile State.

A revival of liberal thinking in terms of the changed circumstances and the expanding sphere of state activity seems therefore most essential if we are to preserve our liberties, if the individual is to maintain even a residue of his personality. The liberalism of the 19th century had no doubt many weaknesses; it was complacent, it took little note of economic factors, equated *laissez faire* with liberty and attached too much importance to the reasonableness of man. And yet it had one supreme virtue: it believed *in the worth of the individual.* The liberal doctrine is built up around the individual, his right to freedom, to be left alone and not to be shaped, moulded and governed too much by others. It is perhaps old-fashioned to talk about the individual, but I would like to emphasise that, however much we may worship the golden calf of the state, praise its virtues and sing its glory, its ultimate justification is only in its service to the individual. The "total view" of society which elevates the organism at the expense of the cells, the whole at the expense of what makes up the whole, denies the fundamental postulates of liberal thinking and is in my opinion an enemy of liberty.

Clearly the liberalism of the 19th century, whatever its value in the circumstances of the time, cannot be revived now. We are living in a different kind of State, in a vastly different political climate and a rapidly changing economy. The conceptions of liberalism, especially those relating to civil liberties, have to be carefuly thought out again and related to the conditions of our time. The omnipotent state cannot be wished out of existence, nor can economic life revert to the jungle of *laissez faire*. But the limitations that these and other factors introduce and render necessary on such conceptions as freedom of speech and association, freedom from arrest except through normal processes of law, etc., have to be examined, and the whole doctrine restated.

The basic conception of liberal politics is the rule of law: the subordination of all authority to the decision of the courts, the free acceptance of law by everyone, from the highest executive authority to the meanest individual. The right of individuals to deny the validity of laws—not the *ukases* or *firmans* of monarchs, or what is imposed on a subject people by a foreign government—is an anarchical doctrine, not a principle of freedom but a denial of freedom. Such action, whether it be deliberate public defiance or a passive refusal to accept, amounts to a repudiation of society. I will not take you into a discussion on whether bad law should be obeyed or whether and in what circumstances civil resistance, which is a form of organised but non-violent rebellion against the State, is justified. Briefly it may be said that resistance to law is justified in the same circumstances as organised rebellion against the State is justified. But it has to be recognised that the substitution of law for force in the relations of men is the basis of civilised society. The extension of the territories of a state to the great continental organisations we have today, whether it be in India, China, the Soviet Union or the U. S. A., is a major development in world history because it brings under one system of law vast masses of people and makes them live in peace. The Rule of Law ensuring at the same time the authority of the state and the liberty of the individual is the hall-mark of the civilised state.

So much will easily be granted. But the New Despotism which the emergence of the bureaucratic state involves and which appears unavoidable with the almost unlimited extension of the power of the paternal state, looking after every aspect of one's life, the much cherished Rule of Law may itself import new terrors to the individual: for the law itself may be transformed over large spheres into administrative authority, and secondly, this is the danger that I am more concerned with, the law-makers may either ignore or forget the obvious fact that laws are meant essentially for the protection of the individual and society and only in exceptional cases for the aggrandisement of the power of the State itself. The tendency of late has been to arm the State with exceptional powers, to encroach on the right of the individual, to give protection to those in authority, and to build up in fact the framework of a servile state.

This dangerous tendency has also infected India. We know of legislation to empower the State to detain persons without trial, to recast the legal system in such a way as to restrict the rights of the accused. I offer no criticism on the specific proposals, each of which may be justified by circumstances, but do they not indicate a tendency to exalt the powers of the State at the expense of the individual? This is something which each one of us has to watch carefully, for in democracy it is the duty and the obligation of each one to safeguard the atmosphere of freedom in which he lives.

It is my conviction that we can safeguard our freedom only by a restatement of the principles of liberalism, with its emphasis on the worth of the individual, with its deep suspicion of the activities of the State in spheres where they encroach on the freedom of individuals and groups, with its faith in humanistic education. The eclipse of liberal thought in India has in my opinion been a misfortune. That eclipse, I am convinced, is not due to any repudiation of the principles which formed the basis of our national life, but as a result of the widened activities of the State, of the immense new responsibilities that the government has had to shoulder, especially in the field of food production, economic and other developments and the urgency of the problem of national security forced on us by the threatening condition of the world we live in. Therefore, it is still possible for us to arrest this dangerous development now before it becomes too late, because the hold of the principles of a liberal society, though weakened by recent developments, is still a part of our mental make-up. To achieve this it is essential that there should be a greater awareness of the dangers of the new tendencies, a fresh realisation of the value of freedom in an independent state, a determination to safeguard our liberties, consistent with the powers and functions of a planning State, determined to secure economic and social advancement for its people.

So far as we of this generation are concerned, we have the assurance that our present leaders, brought up in the tradition of civil liberties, still attach value to them, and though the pressure of the new omnipotent State may now and then seem to gain on them, they can be depended upon not to yield to it easily. But with every passing day the position will become more and more difficult unless the new generation realises the position and is mentally alert to this danger. It is on you and on people like you that the responsibility to safeguard our liberties lies. It is you who have to formulate in your own minds a coherent theory of the relations of the individual to the State, which is what we call our freedom, and uphold it with vigilance. Independence is a great thing: economic prosperity is a most desirable thing, but unless both these can be reconciled with freedom for the individual, life even in an independent and economically prosperous society will mean but little. So my one piece of advice to you is to have faith in freedom, to turn away from those who, whatever their political colouration be, speak disparagingly of freedom and sing the glories of the omnipotent State, able and willing to take care of you from birth to death, who talk as if law did not matter and the necessity of the State was in normal times the final arbiter of an individual's destinies. These false philosophies, many of them attractive and all of them plausible, will mean the end of your freedom, unless you steel your heart to resist them and hold fast to the faith in the individual, his worth, his rights, and his benefit as the final goal of all human activity. This is the charge I would lay on the youth of today.

Technology and the Modern State

I DEEM it an unusual privilege to address the Convocation of the College of Engineering and Technology of the National Council of Education, Bengal. I consider the honour exceptional because of the great and honoured part that the National Council of Education has played in the revival of the Indian mind and the contribution it has made to our national recovery. Very few people remember today the circumstances under which the Council came into existence, the urge for national education, the humiliation that the leaders of the time felt in being dependent solely on an alien government for our intellectual nourishment. The National Council of Education was the first attempt to establish an independent educational system suited to our needs. The names associated with that movement sound today like a roll-call of greatness —to mention only a few, Anand Mohan Bose, Rabindranath Tagore, Gurudas Banerji, Shri Aurobindo, Acharya Prafulla Chandra Ray, men who have immortalised themselves in the history of our country.

I need not emphasise today, when we are free and independent, how important a system of national education is for the preservation of the soul of a people. When the Jews were dispersed by the Romans after the destruction of their Temple the most important decision that the elders of the nation took was to maintain uncontaminated their educational system. For this purpose they established the great centre of Judaic learning at Jabneh. "Give me Jabneh and its scholars",

Address to the National Council of Education, Bengal, 1954.

the great Rabbi Johanan ben Zakkai is reported to have requested Vespasian. When the Romans had destroyed Jerusalem, Jabneh upheld the spirit of Judaism and enabled it to live. In India the problem was not serious till the British began educating us. The Muslim rulers of north India had to a large extent left untouched the Hindu centres of learning with the result that after 600 years of foreign authority the Hindu mind had preserved in a singular degree its special characteristics. But the position was wholly different under the British. The system of education introduced by the East India Company had many advantages; it brought the fruits of New Learning to our doors and helped in a process of cross fertilisation which was responsible for our early recovery. But it had also an ideological bias. To those who could take their minds back to the last century or even to the first decade of the 20th century, the ideological background of our education would now seem to have been strongly anti-Indian. It was a long and wearying paean of praise for everything Western. Its basic theme was the superiority of the West in every sphere. India, we were told, had no art. She had no history. Her achievements were belittled when they could not be wholly denied. The necessity for a scheme of national education, independent of government-controlled schools, was first recognised by the leaders of Bengal, who organised this great association both as a declaration of educational independence and as an act of faith—a first step towards the great ideal they had set before themselves.

Bengal's contribution to India's Recovery, to the growth of national sentiment, is acknowledged by every Indian to have been unique. In almost every sphere of national activity Bengal gave the lead by selfless sacrifices at a time when the rest of India was somnolescent and I am sure that the historian of the future will place high in the list of Bengal's contributions to India its revolt against officialised education, of which the symbol was the establishment of the National Council of Education.

Of the activities and achievements of the Institution sponsored by the Council it is unnecessary for me to speak. The great leaders of the time who were associated with the National Council, while themselves reared in the great traditions of liberal humanism, distinguished lawyers, judges, professors, poets and philosophers, had the foresight to see that what a free India of the future would require were engineers and technicians who would provide, when the time came, the leadership required for building up the country. Your Founding Fathers had a just appreciation of the great role of engineers in the modern world and decided, very wisely, to concentrate their energies on this College of Engineering and Technology—an institution justly famed all over India, not only as the pioneer of technological studies but one which has materially contributed to the industrial advancement of India.

It cannot be said that our age is one which does not extend full and even generous appreciation to technology. In fact it is often described as the age of technology. Some years ago a furious debate raged as to the comparative value of classical and technical studies. Today the pendulum seems to have swung definitely to the side of technical education. The more intelligent section of our youth seems to show a definite preference for scientific studies. In 1948 the number of those who passed the M. A. Examination was 2,127 and out of them only 300 obtained a first class, while out of 765 candidates who passed the M. Sc. Examination as many as 201 secured a first class. By 1952, only a few years later, the position in regard to Arts had further deteriorated to a very serious extent. Out of the 6,036 candidates who passed the M. A. Examination in 1952 only 395 secured a first class, while out of the 1,423 who passed the M. Sc. Examination as many as 358 obtained a first class. This is indeed a revolutionary change, which has attracted but little attention. That scientific and technical subjects are definitely more popular with the better-endowed students of our universities is a major fact, the significance of which requires careful examination.

Human progress or civilisation has always been associated with technical advances. The very names Stone Age, Bronze Age and Iron Age would indicate this. If you examine the

5

different epochs of human history, it will be seen that any advance of civilisation that was registered was due either to new inventions leading to better utilisation of natural resources or to improvements and modifications of the technology of the past leading to a considerable betterment of the material set-up of life. As the historian Wittfogel points out, it was the large-scale utilisation of the waters of the rivers for irrigation that led to the great civilisations of the past in Egypt, in the Tigris Valley, in India, in China and in Peru. It was the ability to build permanent ways of communication, to bring water from distant places for urban use and other superior technology that formed the basis of Rome's civilisation. It is unnecessary for me to press this point as this is almost a historical axiom.

But it would be a great mistake to think, as many people seem to think today, that technology and civilisation are synonymous, and a system of technocracy is therefore the highest form of organised society. A great and fundamental advance in technology divides one age of civilisation from another and provides the basis on which ways of life can be bettered or changed, but it does not by itself constitute civilisation. Continuous modification in technology imperceptibly changes the environments of life and introduces new factors which may slowly lead to a metamorphosis of our accepted conceptions of civilisation. For there is one thing which cannot be emphasised too much, that civilisation is a social state, a condition of human relationships, the prevalence of spiritual and mental qualities in the people as a whole, and not merely an advance in material comforts and greater production of wealth. No one is likely to deny the importance of physical welfare, improved conditions of living and the hundred other things resulting from material prosperity, in the make-up of civilisation. Simple living and high thinking is nothing but the escapist cry of a poverty-stricken people who like to delude themselves that though poor they are superior in mind.

But it needs to be emphasised, especially in our time when scientific and technological revolutions are changing the bases of our lives, that, fundamentally, civilisation is the continuing harmony of all factors which constitute the social life of the community and not merely additional riches and greater advancement in science.

The greatness of a nation and its civilisation will at all times be judged by two factors: first, the contribution it makes to knowledge and the use to which that knowledge is put, and secondly by its contribution to the world of thought and beauty. No country has achieved any kind of greatness in history without an adequate contribution in both these spheres. When we talk of the civilisation of China, Egypt or ancient Greece, we think not merely of the great advances in knowledge associated with them, but also of the poetry, art and architecture they produced and have left as a heritage to humanity, of the quality of their original thinking by which they have helped to shape the thought of the world. Is not the same true of the modern world? The claims of England, France and Germany and the other great nations of our day are equally based on these factors. It is not only increase in scientific knowledge that has proceeded from these countries that places them in the vanguard of civilisation but the treasury of beauty in art, literature and architecture which they have opened to us which justifies their claim to be in the procession of historic nations. It is Shakespeare, Hobbes and Berkely, no less than Newton, Watt and Rutherford that add to the glory of England. France was the leader of civilisation not merely because of her great scientists and inventors, from Descartes to Madame Curie, but also because of her poets, painters and Encyclopaedists. Germany retains her place among the greatest nations even in defeat not merely because of her great industrial power and high technology, but because of Goethe and Schiller, of Kant and Schopenhauer and, let us add, Karl Marx. So it is everywhere.

While therefore it is true that civilisation is by no means a matter exclusively of scientific advancement, I would venture to affirm once again that for any great progress in civilisation scientific advancement is an essential pre-requisite. The march of civilisation is generally by slow and almost imperceptible changes but occasionally it takes a leap which creates a gulf between the immediate past and the present, indicating a qualitative change. Yesterday looks as if it were a hundred years ago, and our own earlier life seems as if it were spent in another age. Such a change which ushers in new eras and new ages is not a common occurrence in history and often the people who live through it have no idea of the significance of the changes that have come into their own lives. The world has been going through such a period during the last fifty years and, to the historian's eye, it is clear enough that we are witnessing a revolution in thought and life such as the world has not seen for the last 450 years. It is of course the cumulative result of centuries of historical progress and yet when it has come it has come with the suddenness of lightning and the consequences of an earthquake. The clearest evidence of it is in the realm of science itself as a noted philosopher has stated:

"Physics, upon which all other sciences must necessarily build, introduces the modern man to new and bewildering if not contradictory concepts. He hears of a finite but unlimited universe, of wrinkled and twisted space and time. He is told of electrons and protons constituting the atom, whirling in unimaginable orbits at inconceivable speeds, and before he has accommodated his mind to their fantastic dances they are joined by neutrons and positrons in a system of which the mathematical framework is still more complicated. If he supposes himself to understand the character of energy—a very foolish supposition on the part of any man—he must add to it the conception of negative energy. He must enlarge his mind to embrace half a dozen geometries which would have made Euclid stare and gasp. He must attempt to visualize cosmic rays, and 'waves of probability' and be aware while he is attending to his income-tax forms that he is a dweller in an exploding or stampeding universe."

All that this means is that science itself has taken some very revolutionary steps forward, which, as we said, is the sign of a change of age and of civilisation which would make our own yesterday look so far away.

If, as I venture to suggest, we are living in an age of Revolution—not the kind of revolutions of which textbooks of history speak, which are changes of political structure accompanied by the roar and thunder of the populace, but a genuine Revolution involving a total break with the past in the sphere of basic thought—then it is necessary that we should try and understand what is happening around us and adjust ourselves to the changing circumstances. A new humanism has to develop on the basis of the changes in our own process of thinking; a new basis of social harmony, a new system of relationships has to be created from the rubble and ruin which we now see around us; for the greatest advances in science will mean nothing unless they are transformed into values.

It is for this reason that I emphasise the necessity of humanistic studies in our technical institutions. Engineers, as I have said before, constitute the advance guard of a new life, because they give practical shape to scientific progress. They utilise and make available to the common man scientific knowledge translated into social values. But if they are to fulfil their high functions properly it is necessary that, apart from attaining a high level of technical knowledge, they must also have a general idea of social purposes and values.

All of us know that progress in every direction depends on science, that even in what appears the most insignificant sphere improvement can come only through the utilisation of scientific knowledge. We must, however, remember that no nation can progress on second-hand science, on the fruits of the labour of others. It is only when a nation by its own efforts contributes its share to scientific advancement that it joins the family of progressive nations. Material developments, industrialisation and other outward forms of progress based on borrowed knowledge are illusory and cannot lead a nation to greatness. The most significant thing in India, after her independence, has been the attention paid by our leaders to the creation of conditions for high-level scientific work. Apart from all other considerations, technology on which we put so much emphasis is dependent on scientific work and its independent progress in India should be based on the work of our scientists. Research, in order to co-ordinate the work of the scientists with that of the technologists, is one of the primary functions to which institutions like yours should be devoted.

To the graduates of this year I would venture to say: you are going out of this institution with your degrees and your diplomas to an India which not only needs you but looks to you and others like you for the early realisation of her dreams. India today is going through an immense process of regeneration. It has been my good fortune to travel over the length and breadth of India, to visit the less frequented areas of the country, to see for myself what is happening. I can assure you, gentlemen, that nothing has gladdened my heart so much as the impression I received wherever I went that we were passing into a period of beneficient revolutionary changes brought about not by blood and thunder but by the quiet and peaceful work of our people. Wherever you go, far south in Tinnevelly or Cape Comorin or in the Himalayas or in the arid plains of Rajasthan, you see great works in progress, immense undertakings, mighty transformations of land such as this country has never witnessed at any time before. I am not alluding merely to the gigantic projects like those at Bakhra-Nangal, Damodar Valley or Hirakud, which are themselves the symbols of the new revolution and which will gladden the heart of every engineer, but programmes in which thousands of villagers, millions of people are involved, which alter the outlook of the common man towards his surroundings and give him fresh hopes and new aspirations. It is a new and in many ways unfamiliar India that is being built up. It is changing not merely the face of our country but the character of our people. It is in this great work of building up that you and others like you, trained in the highest skills and animated by noble social purposes, can play a dominant role. In the mighty drama of effort and experiment that is going on before our eyes, you are called upon to play no mean part.

It is a vision which should move and inspire the most matter-of-fact mind. Our country is no doubt ancient. We are thereby in a position to call forth hidden sources of national vigour, memories of racial greatness in the past, to sustain our strength; but for all that we are also a new nation, with a vision of greatness before our eyes, a greatness different from that of our past in that it is to be built up by the conscious effort of the whole people, by a mighty endeavour to which everyone makes his contribution. It takes the whole of the nation in its purview; includes every part of India in its range; and plans not only for greater wealth but for a better life. It is to this effort that the nation expects you to contribute not merely your technical skill but your enthusiasm born of the hope of a new era of greatness for our country, your enterprise and initiative born of your burning faith in to-morrow. You are alert, keen and have had the best training that India could give. The opportunities are there for you such as those who preceded you did not have. It is for you now to justify the expectations that the country has placed in you. I wish you god-speed in that work.

The Past and the Present

THE ORIGINAL purpose of a Convocation Address, a ceremony of respectable antiquity, was, I presume, to give advice and admonition to the new graduates launching forth on their careers in the world. But as in the case of most ceremonies and rituals, the original purpose has long been forgotten and today it is no more than the observations of an elderly gentleman on some theme of his own choice. I think this change is altogether appropriate, for I do not believe that people of one generation can give advice to those of another. They live in different mental climates, are moved by different ideals, and motivated by different aspirations and hopes. It would therefore, in my opinion, be presumptuous for anyone to offer words of advice or admonition to the new generation.

The theme I have chosen for myself today is the relation of our past, our history, traditions and social heritage to the new life in India. There is no denying that there is a new life in India, a tremendous mental, moral and social effort to create a better way of living. It may not be as revolutionary or as broad-based as some people may desire; its pace may not be as quick, and its results not so spectacular as others may have expected; but it is undoubted that the whole country from Rameswaram to Badrinath and from the Punjab to Assam is throbbing with a new urge, which shows itself not merely in economic, political and other activities, but equally in art, literature, science and other spheres of creative work. I have

Convocation Address to the Agra University, 1955.

had the unique opportunity during the last nine months of travelling extensively in every part of India, of coming into contact with leaders of every section of opinion, young and old, and what impressed me most was the faith of the common man in the better days to come and his desire to contribute to it. Freedom has undoubtedly awakened us from our age-long sloth and put us on the path of hard work, of a burning desire to catch up with the world, to shed the *impedimenta*, the heavy burden of useless accretions, which slowed our movements in the past. The great and mighty process of land transformation, going on in a hundred different ways all over India, the re-organisation of our village life, the improvement of the material setting of life which accompanies electric power to every nook and corner of the country, the power given to the down-trodden and the depressed by adult franchise, these have created a greater revolution than even the changes one sees in the cities, or the steady progress in industrialisation which has been a marked characteristic of our recent life. Taken together, no impartial observer will deny that we are today engaged in a great effort to re-shape our life and re-mould the social and economic patterns of our country in such a way as to create a different and, we all hope, a better world for those who come after us.

But side by side with this I also saw, not with any surprise, as indeed I expected to see it, the crystallisation of reaction, the claims of caste raising their ugly head, shrill cries about the sanctity of animal life, attempts to glorify the past and belittle the present, emphasis on historical greatness of parts as against the whole, a desire in some cases to look back rather than forward. Instead of a desire to see an integrated Indian community pressing forward to greater prosperity and better civilisation, we see, in many parts of India, a vague yearning for the glories of an undefined past. In fact the weight of history seems to lie heavily on us.

The process is of course normal in history, the co-existence of contradictory tendencies in the same communities, often indeed in the same people at the same time. As James Frazer has said, the inconsistency of acting on two opposite principles, however it may vex the philosopher, rarely troubles the common man: indeed he is seldom even aware of it. If we examine our own mental processes and daily habits, we shall no doubt see many such contradictions. While working for a new India based on modern ideals of society, often, unconsciously, we idealise the past, or rationalise our prejudices in favour of indefensible things in our social life. This strange contradiction in our national life is nothing peculiar to us, nothing of which we need be ashamed. But it poses a major problem for the philosopher, for the historian and the sociologist, viz. the rightful place of the past in the present and in the shaping of the future.

History provides some strange instances of attempts made to eradicate the past totally in the evolution of a people. Akhen Aton was perhaps the first of whom we have any knowledge who attempted a radical breach with the past. Chin Shih Huan Ti, the first Emperor of China, ordered the destruction of all books and previous records in the vain hope that a new world could be created by him. All revolutions seem to cherish the belief that the world after them will be something unconnected with the past. The extravagances of the French Revolution in this connection are well known. The Goddess of Reason displaced earlier beliefs and a new era was established and even the names of the months were changed so that there might not be any connection with the past. It is unnecessary to quote other and more recent examples, but in every case that we know the effort proved to be vain. Akhen Aton's reforms did not last, and in spite of the thoroughness with which the first Chin Emperor destroyed everything connected with the past, tradition reasserted itself soon after his death and even the books said to have been destroyed were either forged or brought out from their hiding places to form the basis of a new life. After the blood and thunder of a few years, the old gods were quietly re-established in their niches, no doubt with diminished prestige and sometimes under different names. The French Revolution undoubtedly marks a Great Divide not only in French but in European history, but it is clear that the determined efforts of the revolutionaries to sweep Europe clean of the ideas of the *ancien régime* only achieved a moderate success. No one will be found to deny that today's Europe is the heir to the principles of 1789, no less than to the great traditions of the ages that preceded it. In fact the new and the old have mingled to create the living traditions of Europe.

A complete breach with the past is therefore not possible in history. It is not possible either to ignore or to brush away the power of racial memory and historical traditions, which are the true links that bind generations and maintain the continuity of social life. The almost immeasurable power of social institutions, whether the institution be caste or the church, whether it be the joint family or the great legislative codes, has always to be taken into consideration by those who work for a new life, for they have a strange habit of re-appearing in changed forms and with suitable adjustments. The past is therefore always with us.

How does this continuing influence of the past affect our present attempt to build up a new life in India? In order to answer that question properly it is necessary to understand the true nature of India's revolution and the far-reaching changes and adjustments which, over a period of a hundred and fifty years, have transformed Hindu social thought. From Ram Mohan Roy to Mahatma Gandhi, a succession of great men, in different parts of India, brought about a revolution of thought among our people, thus laying the foundations of our new life. Theirs was a continuing process, a process which cast off dead wood, rooted out a parasitical growth, watered new seeds, and generally infused new spirit even when ancient forms were permitted to remain. They were unable to do more because the machinery of state which could have changed the institutions was not in their hands. Today the position is different. The whole question has been given a new slant and a different emphasis as the people have acquired, after centuries of political subordination and social decay, a new set of values, a new dynamism, a fervent desire to make up for the time that has been lost, in fact a revolutionary outlook. The problem for India is how to canalise the revolutionary impulses and build on them a new society

The social structure under which India lives is, by and large, unrelated to the social values she has now adopted. A society which permits untouchability, which functions within the framework of hereditary castes, which tolerates and sometimes actively encourages primitive and animistic beliefs about the sacredness of special varieties of trees and plants and animals, where cities and locations are considered holy not because they are hallowed by great events but by special divine dispensation, surely a society reared on such beliefs is irrevocably condemned as unsuited to modern times. Does the social conscience of the Hindu mind accept these and other survivals of primitive thought? From the earliest times known to history the best minds in India have protested against them. From Gautama Buddha to Mahatma Gandhi. innumerable leaders of Hinduism have revolted against caste. No religious authority of any kind has been vouchsafed for the practice of untouchability. Innumerable texts point out the foolishness of believing in the sacredness of rivers and the virtue of holy places. And yet our social conscience has not yet mustered sufficient indignation to destroy them.

The reason is simple. It is not because these ideas are associated with our religion that our people cling to them. It is because Hindu society has been on the defensive for over 750 years that our people have come to attach sanctity to practices and habits which a free society would have cast away long ago. The enthronement of social customs—widely different and often conflicting—as orthodox Hinduism, with religious sanction behind it, was in the main the outcome of the political power of Islam. Two reasons contributed to this. The Muslim kings, following the Khalifs, allowed the Hindus to be governed by their own laws through their caste panchayats, which had the result of encouraging an anarchic growth of social customs, each claiming orthodoxy and each asserting its sacred character. Secondly, every society on the defensive withdraws into itself and holds fast to what it has inherited. India produced during the period of Muslim influence great reformers: but their activities resulted only in the creation of new sects, for society as a whole thought it more important to ward off attacks that threatened it by making itself rigid, by refusing to yield an inch for fear of losing a mile, than to reconsider values and re-organise social life. It is only a free society that can undertake large-scale reforms.

One basic fact has to be remembered when we examine the question of the relationship of the past with the present, and it is that the social organisation of the Hindus is the result of unregulated growth which, through historical reasons, got stunted in its early stages. The problem facing us today may therefore be formulated as a re-thinking of social values, a re-organisation of social institutions and a divorce between law and custom on the one hand and religion on the other. It is only when this is done through legislation, affecting Hindus of all sects and all communities through the length and breadth of India, that it will be possible for us to examine seriously the integration of our past traditions with the present.

The legislative measures relating to Hindu social life now under consideration of Parliament are the first cautious steps in this direction. They seek to regulate Hindu marriage and inheritance laws, to permit marriages between different castes, to legalise divorce, and to provide inheritance rights for women. It is not my purpose to discuss these laws but to draw attention to the fact that it is the first attempt to transform the Hindus from a conglomeration of small units into a community, a single people, united by common social ideals and bonds. Religious doctrines and dogmas cannot be changed as they are *ex hypothesi* immutable, but secular society must undergo continuous adjustments if it is to survive. A continuous and vigorous criticism of social trends and a revaluation of customs and practices and their modification to suit changing conditions of life—these are the charateristics of a living society.

It is true that throughout Indian history there have been attempts to re-organise Hindu social life. The difference between such movements in the past and in the circumstances of today lies in two very important facts. The first is that the vast majority of the Hindu people is now, for the first time in history, united under a single political authority. The second, which is no less important, is that this political authority is armed with a legislative and judicial machinery competent to enact and enforce basic social legislation. In every age, since at least the time of the Buddha, there have been vigorous movements for reform in Indian society. In fact it would be no exaggeration to say that India's claim to civilisation is not based so much on her social institutions as on her movements of protest against those institutions. From Gautama Buddha to Mohandas Gandhi, it is an imposing array of men that India can claim to have produced to combat the evils of her social institutions. But these great men, though they gave expression to the protests of national conscience, did not have the machinery of the organised state to give effect to their reforms. The principle of social obedience in India remained familial and local and Hinduism continued to live much in the same way in spite of her great men.

But the point I desire to emphasise today in relation to my main theme of the connection between the past and the present is that the dominant intellectual tradition of our past is one of unorthodoxy and protest. This may sound paradoxical in relation to a community which calls its religion Sanatana Dharma. But if we examine events closely we shall see that those whom the orthodox and the Sanatanis honour most today were declared heretics in their own time. The great Sankara, from whom all the Jagadgurus claim apostolic succession, was in his time denounced as a Prachanna Bauddha or a concealed Buddhist. The founder of Vaishnava orthodoxy was accused of raising low-caste people to Brahminhood. In fact Mahatma Gandhi himself, in our own days, was in the same way attacked by the orthodox as being a concealed Christian. I often wonder when reading the Bhagavat Gita whether the orthodox Sanatanists of the day did not denounce Shri Krishna himself for being sarcastic about Veda Vādaratas (people who delight in discussing the Vedas) whose flowered speech (Pushpitām vacham) Arjuna was enjoined to reject utterly. Thus the tradition of criticism, protest and free enquiry into the postulates of social order are as much a part of our tradition as blind clinging to irrational customs and social abuses.

Now it is obvious to all except those who dream vainly of a golden past and whose vision is turned backwards that the problem of problems before India is to ensure that the great material revolution that is taking place today is co-ordinated and harmonised by an equivalent progress in our social thinking. It is for this generation in India to discover and effectively realise the methods of social action which will eradicate the disharmonies of our life and provide for a continuous re-valuation and adjustment as a normal process. It was the great philosopher Auguste Comte who emphasised the basic relation between the material aspects of living and social institutions and this truth has been further emphasised by the present advance of science and technology in our every-day life. The inherited institutions under which we live today postulate a practically self-sufficient rural society: a system of life in which relationships are localised. The economy it visualises is that of subsistence agriculture and hereditary handicrafts. Though this economic system broke down in cities and towns with the growth of industrialisation it had till recently retained sufficient life in our villages to prevent the growing contradictions of our life from coming too much to the surface. Life in the rural communities appeared superficially at least to flow normally and without too many crises. But the last seven years of independence have changed all that. We have carried revolution to the villages. The new economy we are trying to develop is based not merely on large-scale industrialisation in cities, but on the message of science and technology carried to the remotest villages. What are our Community Projects and National Extension Services but an attempt to urbanise our village life and introduce into the heart of the rural society not only the methods and techniques which improve the economy but also new principles of social life and activity which go against the very conception of village society? For the first time in Indian history, the village is on the march. For thousands of years it had been left undisturbed. Political revolutions, barbarian invasions and foreign rule had touched it but little. But today it is learning new methods of production, new habits of living, and developing new bonds of social life. In fact it is losing its identity as a village. It is going through a revolution creating an unbridgable gulf between its past and its future. That it is a deliberately planned and consciously directed process of change does not make it the less a revolution. Further, it is a continuing process, for these changes once started gather momentum and move forward till society finds a new level. It is to the character and tempo of this revolution that our past, which is represented by our social institutions, has to be adjusted.

The gravest danger to a society comes when material progress outstrips the progress of social thinking, when prosperity, increase in wealth, and all that goes with it, are not reflected in social conscience. True there is always a time lag but it should be the conscious effort of democratic leadership to bridge the time lag and continuously to modify and adjust our social ideals and our behaviour to enable the spiritual growth of people—I use the words in the widest sense—to keep pace with material advancement. I see the greatest danger to our future not so much in our military weakness, or our political inefficiency, or the slow rate of our economic progress—all these are no doubt alleged by critics—but positively in the crystallisation of social reaction over wide groups and negatively in the abscence of a revolutionary urge in regard to the re-building of our society commensurate with the new urges of our economic life.

The past will remain with us, for no one could deny wholly his own national and racial inheritance. But it is for us in each generation to reject so much of our past as has become a dead weight and to encourage and develop such of it as fits in with our conceptions of life today. The dirt and dust of dead customs which we, through lack of unified authority, allowed to accumulate in our ancient family house has now to be cleared if we mean to live a clean and healthy life. That the mansion itself is habitable in spite of its dust heaps and has at all times had a minimum of light, air and drainage is amply demonstrated by the fact that we have continued to live within its four walls for so long a time. That kind of living does not satisfy us today. We want to lead a healthier, cleaner and happier life. The ancient mansion has not only to be cleaned up and the accumulated dust heap of ages swept away vigorously, but new openings for light and air, modern drainage and sanitary arrangements and even air conditioning have become necessary, for the Indian people are determined to live as equals of others in the world and are no longer content to live in a dirty present with the dreams of a golden past.

Social reaction is the enemy we have to face. It takes many forms and shapes and speaks in many voices. Sometimes it appears in the dream image of a golden age; sometimes in the pious but deceptive robes of a religious teacher; more often and dangerously as a modern-minded cynic criticising the evils of today and undermining our faith in progress; but the common characteristic by which the enemy, however disguised, can be spotted is his dislike of the present. The language which he speaks may be equally different. It may be that of astrology, of spiritualism or of *smriti*. It may use the jargon of art, literature and culture. It may even intone the phrases of the most recent philosophical thinking, of existentialism and all other variations of human despair. But, again, whatever the language he uses, the enemy can be spotted by his desire to discredit and his anxiety to undermine our hope of a better future.

All I say to the youth of the nation is Be On Guard. Be careful that out of a sense of frustration and sometimes out of a false sense of superiority you do not slip into these dangerous ways of thinking. If the youth of a nation loses faith in its future, then that nation is irrevocably lost. Therefore I say again, honour the past, but look to the future: accept from the past what is good for today, but do not carry on your shoulders the weight of a dead past. It is for you to make the future of India, and that future will, I am sure, be better than any golden age of which you may have been told.

On National Unity

THE RAJASTHAN area has been for centuries considered the home of lost causes. Its desert character combined with the valour of its people enabled it to preserve in a large measure its political independence and its special ways of life. It was the recognised home of chivalry where the *charans* sang the glories of a great past. It was a land where ancient romance still lingered, picturesque, colourful and remote. The forts and castles, the palaces and *killas* which raise their proud heads here and there in the vast and barren desert aroused in us the pride in a heroic period in our history. It was and still is an area famed all over India in song and legend.

Today all this is undergoing a change, for we are living in an era of mighty transformation. The main, and I should think, distinguishing characteristic of the period we live in is Change. It is not merely change in one sphere or another but in all aspects of human life, in the realm of ideas, no less than in the realm of action, in social organisation, no less than in economic life. This increased tempo of change, giving to our age a revolutionary character, may be seen in all parts of the world, in the developments now taking place everywhere. But nowhere has it been more striking than in India. And even in this country, nowhere has it been more revolutionary, more basic, more far-reaching than in Rajasthan. Cast your mind back eight years and try to recapture by imagination the life in Rajasthan before 1948, and you will realise how far away we have moved from that time. We

Address to the Rajputana University, 1955.

were then living in a society based on status, when people attached importance to such matters as *tazeem*, the wearing of gold on their ankles, and other similar honours. The tradition of political life was monarchical and authority was derived from the Ruler himself. The claim of paramountcy cast its shadow over the entire area, subjecting the rulers and the people alike to its blighting effects. Today all this has vanished. The hierarchical society is no longer there. *Tazeems* and other honours, so prized but a decade ago, mean nothing now to anyone and the age-old tradition which related to political power, to the possession of land, has disappeared. Though these changes are but recent, the age that has passed seems far away. Though in time the distance is not great, the ideas appear, even to us, as of another age, of long ago, for the *ancien régime* has become truly a thing of the past, and in the world of ideas what is discarded becomes not merely unfamiliar but something which is utterly strange and often repelling.

If we examine carefully the period in which our life has been cast, it will be seen that the most revolutionary fact about it is our attitude towards Change. In India—and indeed in Asian countries generally—the accepted view of society was as a static condition based on immutable principles and on unchanging institutions. Sanatana Dharma or the immutable law was the name by which the Hindus described their own religious society. The idea of change was therefore equated with decline, a fall from moral standards, and therefore had to be resisted at all costs. The idea of progress, of a re-examination of social institutions and of the evolution of society was not generally recognised in the eastern way of thinking. This had for long been a marked feature of Indian life. Reformers of the past and radical thinkers took good care to emphasise that what they were preaching had the authority of *Sruti* or of the *Vedas*. So change was always camouflaged by the fiction of being a restoration to the original doctrine. Even Ram Mohan Roy, the first great modern mind in India, justified the changes for which he pleaded by an appeal to the Upanishads.

Not only in our social and religious approach but in our attitude to the physical world, we held the view that everything was in a static condition. Look at our celebration of equinoxes for example. We still go on celebrating these days, as if the sun reached the meridian on the day we fixed for it thousands of years ago. The many contradictions in our beliefs and attitudes arise from the fact of our refusal to recognise in practice the changes we accept intellectually. Today the position is fast changing. The last half a century has witnessed a revolutionary change in our material conceptions of the world. Every day, even our basic conceptions of space, time, matter and energy are being challenged. Every day brings new discoveries in these fields to which we have to adjust our minds. This revolutionary change in the field of ideas cannot but have its effect on social institutions and economic life, for nothing is more certain than the fact that institutions and ideas are so closely inter-related that, when there is a great movement forward in ideas, institutions must inevitably change.

Consequently the last half a century in India has seen a remarkable transformation in our approach to many problems. Our national movement, which achieved the freedom of the country, reflected in many respects this change in our ideas. I have only to mention the question of untouchability and the attitude towards women to prove how fundamental are the changes that the national movement brought about in the minds of our people.

The growth of the scientific approach, as a result of the revival of scientific studies, also helped to gain wide acceptance for the doctrine of change. India's contribution in the domain of higher physics, chemistry and mathematics during the last half a century has not been negligible, but much more important than the achievements of our scientists has been the scientific approach to our daily problems like public health, sanitation, child welfare, etc. which has brought home to the ordinary men and women the knowledge that change is in the nature of things.

Today the villager in India not only accepts change, but

clamours for it. Not only does he want change in the material set-up of life but he is prepared to question all the concepts which he had blindly accepted before as immutable laws: caste, joint family, sacramental marriage, enforced widowhood, etc. The patent fact that our economic life is undergoing vast and previously inconceivable changes, transforming the ancient pattern of our life, that science and modern techniques are revolutionising the conditions of material existence, has made even the most ignorant man in the villages realise that everything is changing. He has in fact come to understand that change is not something which has to be resisted automatically.

One practical aspect of this acceptance of the doctrine of change in the political field with which everyone in India is concerned at the present moment is the territorial reorganisation of India which seeks to rationalise the state structure of our federation. It is a subject which has, as is but right, led to a Great Debate in our democracy. Fundamental changes in a country which believes in democratic institutions cannot be imposed on a people. They can only be brought about successfully after prolonged discussion in which every citizen has a right to participate. The Great Debate now taking place all over India, where every kind of view is being expressed freely and frankly, provides irrefutable evidence of the strength of democratic institutions in India, which seek to bring about fundamental changes by a process of moral suasion, free discussion, and honest criticism. As one who was, no doubt to a very small extent, responsible for the proposals under discussion now, it is not for me to participate in the controversy; but one fundamental postulate in our Report I should like to emphasise here. To us on the Commission,* as I believe to everyone else in India, the governing fact in our political life is the primacy of the Union, the overriding importance of the concept of a single Indian nation, the supreme imperative of upholding and strengthening the

* The States Reorganization Commission was appointed by the Government of India on 29 December 1953, with Shri Fazl Ali as Chairman and Pandit H. N. Kunzru and Sardar K. M. Panikkar as Members.

unity of the country. It is with us only the Union that is indestructible and should be considered indestructible. It is only to the unity of India that sanctity should be attached. There is no sanctity, and there should be none, attached to territorial boundaries or to the composition of the units which, according to our economic, administrative and other requirements, should always be subject to adjustment. The idea that there is any special virtue in units, whether they be called Travancore or Mysore, Uttar Pradesh or Madhya Pradesh, for instance, is something which no patriotic Indian can countenance. The survival of such parochial loyalties is in my opinion something which should be rooted out, however much political romanticists might glory in them. What is there more sacred or valuable in these states than in the great states that have already vanished, than in Udaipur with its past tradition of unbending patriotism, than in Kolhapur with its tradition of Maratha revival, than in Baroda with its tradition of enlightened modernism? If they can disappear as states from the map of India, what is it that is special which we should cherish in other states?

Nor can we countenance the idea that special sanctity attaches to states' boundaries because of Vardhamana and Buddha, Rama and Krishna, Sankara and Madhva, or other great personalities. No state or area can claim them as its own. They belong to the whole of India and not merely to the area where they were born and claims based on special association with these great figures can only be considered fantastic. This kind of thinking can only weaken our sense of one-ness and it is in my opinion more dangerous than even the claim based on languages.

The essential thing to remember is that in a modern state economic activity has inevitably to cut across political boundaries. In the days of village economy we could think of even districts as units of economic life; but today everywhere in the world economic activity has to transcend local boundaries. Nowhere is this more so than in India. All our great river valley schemes affect a number of states. The Bhakra Dam and the irrigation and power system based on it will transform not merely the Punjab, but areas in Rajasthan. The Damodar Valley Project relates to Bihar and to Bengal. The great national industries now being located in different states, the fertiliser plant at Sindri, the Rourkela steel plant, the Perambur integral coach factory, the Chittaranjan locomotive factory and many others are financed by the Centre and will benefit India as a whole. In fact, the utilisation of the resources of each area for the benefit of all is the basis of national planning and, therefore, all-India economic thinking cannot afford to take undue notice of provincial considerations. This is true all the world over. The Schuman Plan for steel is the best example of integrated economic thinking, because it goes even further and brings under international authority and control iron and steel production in Western Europe. Even in the United States, where the forces of state particularism are strong and firmly rooted, the great developments associated with the Tennessee Valley Authority over-ride state boundaries. In India we can see that these forces are already at work, and the planned economy to which we are wedded takes us far beyond local considerations. Few rivers in India flow through a single State. All the raw materials of any particular industry are seldom available in one State. The Sindri factory is dependent on the gypsum of Rajasthan. Industry all over India is mainly dependent on coal from Bengal and Bihar. In fact the whole economy of India is interdependent. It is our good fortune that an area, continental in resources and in size, in man-power and in variation of climates, has been united under one authority, and this has enabled us to plan for a better future. It should be the duty of each one of us to see that the union which has been brought about is strengthened, and the integration of the different areas becomes more and more effective as each day passes. This is the primary duty of the present generation.

Our political unity is a tender plant of recent growth, the result of our faith in a common life and in a common tradition, brought home to us as a result of a century and a half of foreign rule. The future we visualise for ourselves is bound up with that unity, for if that unity breaks, or even weakens, all our dreams of a better economic life, a freer social atmosphere, and a more respected political position in the world will vanish like dreams. So the tendency which is manifesting itself here and there to lay emphasis on state rights and on regional claims is something which we must vigorously put down, for the only loyalty which we can tolerate at our present stage of development is loyalty to the Union, to India as such.

I should not like to be misunderstood. Regionalism is something which is valuable, so long as the over-riding loyalty to the nation is not only conceded but cherished as a faith. In a country, say, like the United States, England or France, where there is no question of anyone remotely denying the bonds of national unity, it may even be desirable to encourage regionalism for the sake of a richness and variety of culture. But in India, where the sense of unity is new and still not very strong, we cannot afford to encourage ancient loyalties or, through romantic readings of history, to cherish a dual patriotism. Our patriotism today has to be exclusive, directed solely to the strengthening of our unity, to the elimination of all tendencies which weaken our sense of nationality.

I have spoken at some length on this question because, in my opinion, this is the one lesson which the youth of today has to learn. Rajasthan is traditionally a land of romance, a land inclined to live on its past glory, on its heroic memories. As an inspiration for the future, such an attitude can be of value, but romanticism which turns its eyes backwards and exalts the past over the present is a dangerous thing today. We have to look steadily to the future. We have to think not of our past glory, but of our future greatness, and that greatness can come only on the basis of hard work, inspired by an impelling desire to see India march forward. In order to do this, we should be prepared to cast aside our prejudices and our enervating social customs, to forget those traditions that create division among ourselves, to cherish those which strengthen our unity and our strength. With some knowledge of conditions in Rajasthan I can say that in my opinion nowhere is this attitude more necessary than here, for there lingers still in the minds of most people not merely a romantic view of your past, but a vigorous feeling of belonging to separate areas within the state itself. History, clannish, local and dynastic is too much with you yet. There is still the feeling of belonging to Udaipur, Jaipur, Jodhpur and Bikaner and other states of the past. There is hardly yet the feeling of belonging to Rajasthan. The traditions of those great states were in many ways glorious and there is no harm in being proud of them. But let me emphasise once again that while you should be proud of them, you should not forget that the days of separate, independent states in India have gone, never to return, and it is your privilege now to belong to a great state with a common tradition into which all these past glories have merged. Though I come from the southernmost part of India, I claim equally to be an inheritor to the unbending heroism of Rana Pratap, to the administrative and military achievements of Man Singh, and to the high-souled loyalty of Durga Das. They are no longer your local heroes; they are the heroes of India.

Here in Rajasthan, where the past and the present meet and are, I trust, happily blended, the ideal conditions may be said to exist for developing a centre of Sanskrit studies. For over 400 years, Rajasthan was the refuge of Sanskrit scholarship. It is at the courts of Rajasthan that the poets and writers of later Sanskrit flourished. Many rulers like Rana Kumbha of Mewar, Maharaja Ram Singh of Jaipur and Maharaja Anup Singh of Bikaner were eminent scholars and poets themselves. It is through their munificence and patronage that much of the learning of the past came to be preserved. The royal libraries of Jaipur and Bikaner, the famous collection of Jaisalmer and at the other Rajputana courts were the repositories of Indian literature and learning. A glance at the Kavya Mala series published under the editorship of the celebrated scholar, Pandit Durga Prasad of Jaipur, will show how greatly India is indebted to the collection of His Highness the Maharaja for the revival of interest in Sanskrit literature. With so rich an inheritance and with so noble a tradition of encouragement to classical learning, it is but natural to expect that this new university should become an all-India centre of Sanskrit learning. Many people seem to hold the view that in New India, so definitely orientated towards modern studies, scientific, technological and other, the study of Sanskrit can be allowed to take a secondary place. This, in my opinion, is a very short-sighted view. The basis of our cultural unity. is Sanskrit. It is the literature that is embodied in that great language that provides us all over India with the background of our culture. It is to the classics of that language that our traditions are to be traced. Without the continued cultivation of Sanskrit by the intelligentsia of the country, the cultural unity of India will suffer. It is a matter of great satisfaction that there has been a general realisation of the value of Sanskrit studies during the last few years. Rajasthan is particularly suited to take the leadership in these studies. You have magnificent collections of Sanskrit books in almost every former capital and a unique one in the Royal Library in Jaipur. You have a living tradition of Sanskrit scholarship which has contributed so much to the popularisation of Sanskrit. I would venture to suggest that this university should utilise the ample facilities that exist to organise a vigorous school of classical studies, encompassing within its fold both Jain and Hindu traditions.

Freedom is not merely the elimination of foreign rule. To equate it with merely the recovery of our national independence is to forget its more positive aspects, more especially social and economic freedom, freedom of thought, the ensuring of our liberties in general, the possibility of a rich, varied and full life for the individual. We have achieved our independence. We are striving hard to achieve our freedom. We are shaking off, one by one, the shackles that bound us in the past, in the social and economic fields no less than in the field of ideas and action. This is our continuing struggle and with a free nation it is a struggle that can never be allowed to slacken. If a nation becomes complacent about its freedom, it will surely lose it one way or the other. So, each one of you, be you a warrior in this noble cause of enlarging our freedom and upholding our unity. Let me emphasise once again that these two, freedom and unity, are inter-twined to such a degree that without the one we could not have the other. Without freedom our unity would be nothing to us, would only be an unbearable burden. Without unity our freedom cannot be enlarged or even be maintained. This is the one supreme message which we of an older generation can transmit to you. It is for you to take over the torch, hold it aloft and carry it forward.

On Historical Studics

DURING the last half a century much progress has been made in historical studies in India. Notable work has been done on almost every period of Indian history. The history of South India, barely known fifty years ago, has now taken its legitimate place in the story of India. The former bias, based on the dependence of European scholars on the chronicles of Muslim historians is now almost gone, and the greatness of the Pallavas, Chalukyas, Cholas, Pandyas and Ballalas and of the Vijayanagar Empire takes its place with that of their contemporary north-Indian kings. Again, we know much more today about the social life of India during these great periods, and the continuing process of archæological excavations, and the collection and interpretation of epigraphical records is filling up the undoubted gaps that still exist. The history of the Marathas and the Moghuls has been studied in great detail. The earlier imbalance in the history of medieval India mainly resulting from too great a dependence on Muslim annals has also to some extent been rectified.

For some time now, Indian historical work has mainly been local, specialised, and related to dynasties and kings of particular regions. Consequently Indian history has acquired a reputation of being dull and uninteresting. Indian history, if one viewed it as the growth of a people and their existence in time as a civilised community in contact with other peoples and civilisations, is an enthralling subject; but viewed from the political point of view, it is dull, confusing and dreary.

Presidential address to the Indian History Congress, 1955.

The reason for this confusion and lack of sustained interest is that at no time previously to our own day did India achieve political unity. While the unity of Indian culture and its integration within a defined territorial limit has been one of the major factors of world history at least from the 6th century B.C. and was recognised as such by her sister civilisations of Greece, Persia and China, politically India was, till recently, a country of many states and warring dynasties, whose persistent urge towards unity was defeated by geographical factors. The history of India has therefore to be a history of social growth and development and not primarily a political history.

Regular dynastic histories from contemporaneous sources were written only after Muslim rulers established their sway in north India at the beginning of the 13th century. Literary works like *Bana Charita*, *Rajatarangini*, *Vikramanka Deva Charita* and *Prithwi Raja Vijaya*, though they contain much authentic historical material, could not legitimately be considered as histories. For the period before the Muslim invasions we have to depend on inscriptions, epigraphic records and literary compositions. With the establishment of Muslim power in Delhi, we have definite political chronicles but they deal only with warfare and domestic revolutions and are so overlaid with religious fanaticism and prejudice that their value as source books for a history of India is greatly diminished. Also, to them Indian history began only with the arrival of Islam in India. It is only during the period of British authority that histories of India as a whole come to be written. Through a study of foreign sources, Greek, Persian and Chinese, through archæology, numismatics, epigraphical researches and the decipherment of old inscriptions, European scholars were able to create a chronological and dynastic framework for Indian history. But their approach to historical writing, coloured by the national histories of their countries, was purely political. Numerous dynasties were unearthed. A variety of eras adding confusion to our chronology came to light. Empires and kingdoms were re-established in their glory and Indians began to talk of the Mauryas, the

Vakatakas and the Guptas as national monarchs, whose imperial traditions were continued through a succession of dynasties, to create a national entity known to us as Bharatavarsha.

But this approach of European historians suffered from a fatal defect. They could only think of history as a record of the political growth of a nation, on the analogy of Britain, France or Spain evolving into states through the activities of a dynasty, and not as the record of a people living as an integrated civilisation but under dispersed political power. They personified the states and conceived history as the biography of this collective personality. Speaking of the great French historian Michelet, Benedetto Croce recalls his "fantastic idolisation of France as a physical, intellectual and moral person". This judgement is true of most national historians, Treitschke in Germany, Macaulay, Froude and Freeman in England. The school of history which the British historians developed in India, seeing India only as a geographical name and not as a political unit, could not personify her, with the result that they never went beyond the stage of local and dynastic chronicles, with no central connecting link to unify them.

The integration of Indian society and civilisation has until recent times been unrelated to political events and was certainly unconcerned with political unity. It was Dean Inge who described Hinduism as a noncorporeal state, an organisation of society above and beyond the political structure. Whether this is wholly true or not, it is undoubtedly true that a history of the Indian people cannot be written in mainly political terms.

So far we have been engaged in chasing the will-o'-the-wisp of political unity in Indian history, by tending to identify individual dynasties and empires with this ideal and by trying to create around them the image of an Indian nation, an ideal of unity which they were endeavouring to realise. It is difficult to see such a motive in our history. The unity of the civilisation, culture and society of India was assumed at all times but the unity of India as a nation is a recent concept and the attempt to read back into Indian history a permanent motivation which was not only absent, but which would have seemed to most people unnatural, is at the root of our failure in the historical field.

The first requisite therefore to a re-writing of the history of the Indian people is to shed the conception of history which was prevalent in Europe until recent times, as the record of the growth and activities of the nation state. In the particular circumstances of Western European countries it was only natural that their histories which cover comparatively short periods should have been identified with their growth and development as independent nations and should therefore have been concerned with wars and conquests and with the achievements of parliaments and ministries. But even in Europe the growing realisation of the unity of European life and culture has led to a wider conception of history, as a record of the growth of European civilisation in a world context. This school may be said to have originated with Burckhardt whose lectures at Zurich showed how European history had a unity beyond and above the history of individual nations and that too great an emphasis on the history of states led to a falsification of perspective. Since his time and no doubt also as a result of an increasing realisation of the identity of Europe as a single unit in contrast to the Islamic world, Asia and the fast growing communities of America, historians in Europe have to a large extent discarded the national and purely political view which had for so long dominated historical writing. In England, this tendency owed much to the personality of Acton, a truly international figure, a Catholic English aristocrat, connected as closely with Italy and Germany as with England. Acton's one ambition, as every student of history knows, was to a write a history of liberty, a dream which it was not given to him to realise. But as a Catholic and a Dalberg and as the grandson of a Prime Minister of Naples he saw Europe as a single civilisation and he was able through the cooperative histories which he promoted to infuse into English historical studies a sense of European unity. It is significant to note that some of the most outstanding work done in England during the last quarter of a century deals with Europe and not with England. I have only to mention such names as Eileen Power, F. M. Powicke and Christopher Dawson to prove the point. On the continent of Europe the tendency has been much more pronounced. Henri Pirenne who may be considered the greatest of modern historians in his *Mahommed and Charlemagne* deals not with countries but with two confronting civilisations.

An equally interesting development is the new school of history at the university of Paris which is associated with the distinguished name of Fernand Brandel. Brandel's epoch-making work is on the Mediterranean world in the time of Philip the Second. It is a history of a basic region of political, religious, economic and cultural development, and, around the sea and the countries which enclose it, the historian builds up the living picture of peoples' movements, conflict of culture and trade. The attempt is to take history away from territorial grooves and to conceive of it as something related to an integrated civilisation.

I mention these facts to show how Europe has already discarded the idea of confining history within national boundaries and enlarged it to include an entire civilisation. In India we, however, continue to cherish the old ideas and limit ourselves to the history of local dynasties, or attempt the impossible in the search for an imperial unity of India. Both I need not say are fraught with grave dangers. The study of local dynastic histories, without reference to the conditions of India as a whole has led us to the exaggerations of local patriotism which is one of the most dangerous tendencies in India today. Every local historian desires to prove that his area was a leading centre of civilisation and culture from the beginning of time; that the dynasts of his region were great empire builders. In fact, as a result of our localised studies we have come to develop a rivalry in historical greatness. Each area has begun to boast of conquerors and *grand monarques*. The glory of the Cholas and the Pandyas are claimed by the Tamils, of the Satavahanas, Eastern Gangas, Kakatiyas and in a measure of Vijayanagar are claimed by the Andhras. The Kannadigas are not to be considered a lesser people. In fact, from one end of India to the other every region considers its own history as something specially important, something which enables it to claim superiority over its neighbour. This kind of historical study exalts localism based on dynasties and helps in effect to deny the idea of Indian unity, for, however much we might try, we could not establish from history that the political unity of India was ever achieved before. The chasing of the will-o'-the-wisp of Indian nationhood through the labyrinth of time has thus resulted only in the creation of regional jealousies and rivalries.

No one would deny that this kind of history which concentrates on conquests and wars by local heroes develops strange feelings of superiority. But surely in India there is no such variation of talent, such differences in natural endowment, such clearly marked distinctions of character as to enable any region to claim a permanent superiority over others. And yet such has been the result of our studies in local history.

It is time we also discarded finally this attempt to build our history on monarchs and dynasties, and viewed it from the point of view of the evolution of the Indian people. As Professor Maitland observed, history today has lengthened, deepened and widened in nature and scope with the help of archæology, anthropology and sociology.

If, as I believe, the history of a people lies in their social, economic and mental evolution through the ages, then the material for it lies not merely in the discoveries of archæologists and epigraphists—though these are undoubtedly very important—but in the literary records of the people. These are continuous, produced in successive periods and reflect the mind of the period generally more than the conscious records of kings and emperors. A most distinguished military historian, Capt. Liddell Hart, pointed out to me recently the curious fact that the despatches of successful generals, no less than of defeated ones, often contain distortions of fact, and imaginative descriptions of circumstances from which it is difficult to extract truth. It is of course known that *prasasthis* or descriptions in praise of a ruler are seldom trustworthy in regard to facts. Literary evidence is far more dependable as reflecting the temper and character of an age. Even if the incidents narrated are altogether fictitious the circumstances described should help us to understand the life of the period. To quote only one or two instances; in the *Katha Sarit Sagara,* recurring allusions to aboriginal tribes in the Vindhya area generally indicate that the Bhilla kings used to carry out human sacrifice to please the mother goddess. In *Sakuntala* the police inspector who is offered a pourboire by the fisherman invites him for a drink at a tavern—a very significant fact which clearly proves two things: that the use of intoxicating liquor was a normal habit, and that the taverns where caste *tabus* were not strictly adhered to were a feature of urban life. So far only the Vedas have been subjected to this kind of study. But I am sure that if a systematic research is undertaken in Sanskrit and Prakrit literature and in the vast and almost unexplored region of Jain writings we shall discover ample material for a social history of different areas. Again, the *dharma sastra* literature which is so rich and comprehensive and practically comes up to our own time has to be studied as material for history. Dr. Kane's monumental volumes show how rich we are in this field and yet their utilisation as historical material has been very limited.

Viewed from the point of view of the continental character of our history, and the absence of a central national theme, we have, in my opinion, to reformulate the problems on which to concentrate our attention. Of course any attempt to do this does not and should not mean a neglect of political history on a regional basis as before. A few of the questions to which the historian of the Indian people now vainly seeks an answer may be stated here mainly as illustrating my point. The first and most important problem which faces the historian of India is the still uncompleted fact of penetration through the ages of a dominant culture over the vast aboriginal population. Our pre-occupation with the Aryans has led us in a measure to equate Indian social development with the Aryanisation of the country. But it is clear from every available record that from the earliest days the Aryan and the non-Aryan had mingled sufficiently to influence each other and to create a joint culture, which we may well describe as Hinduism. But vast areas even in northern India continued to be occupied by the aboriginal population living in their tribal organisations. A recent study by Dr. Sastri Bhushan Chaudhuri shows how widely spread was the distribution of these tribes which gradually had become Hinduised. The slow evolution of the Indian people from this vast conglomeration of tribes by the imposition of a common Hindu culture is the primary fact of Indian history and should be the subject of major research. That such Hinduisation was a slow process, which continues even today, is established by the existence of many areas predominantly peopled by the tribal groups—especially in the uplands to the south of the Gangetic Valley. The Santals, the Gonds, the Sabaras and the numerous other tribes which constitute a major section of the population of this area are, as we know from their languages, social structure, and tribal traditions, still, in the main, outside the sphere of Hindu life. In the Deccan and in South India, the difference between the Aryan Hindus and the aboriginal population was less, as there was much less of Aryan penetration and the champions of Hinduism would themselves seem to have been Hinduised indigenous peoples.

Another major problem to which Indian historians have to devote their attention is the origin and development of Hindu social institutions and the extent of their prevalence. Again, we have been inclined to think in terms of the universality of Hindu laws and social institutions. This would not bear analysis. Apart from the large population of indigenous tribes, even among the communities which are accepted as orthodox, practices vary very widely. Thus for example even among some Brahmin communities in the south the marriage with an elder sister's daughter is considered orthodox while it is prohibited by every school of Hindu law. Post-puberty marriage is the rule among the orthodox Nampudiri Brahmins of the West Coast. Dr. Irawati Karve has recently established by a scientific study that kinship organisation among the

Marathas shows clear evidence of non-Aryan survivals. In order to study the evolution of the Hindu people, it is necessary therefore that we should extend the scope of our researches.

Changes in ideas is another fascinating subject which is of vital importance to an understanding of Indian history. When did Indians generally begin to consider travel across the sea as something which is unorthodox? That so late as the 11th century there was no social stigma attached to sea voyages is well attested by the continuous flow of people from all parts of India to the countries of South East Asia, by the hundred years war on the seas carried on by the Cholas against the maritime empire of Srivijaya and the Chola occupation of Kataha. In the *Katha Sarit Sagara* a very large number of stories deal with the activities of traders who sailed to *dwipantaras.* But at some undetermined date Hindu society seems to have enforced a *tabu* on sea voyages. Has it any connection with the Muslim-Arab control of the Eastern Seas which became effective at about this time?

Another problem that faces the student is the decadence which seems to have overtaken Hindu society in the period between the 8th and the 12th centuries. That there has been a marked decadence over large areas is well attested by facts. Our architecture, literature, scientific thought and all other spheres of activity proclaim loudly not only a decay of taste and interest but a change of attitude which is truly remarkable. From the simple beginnings of the early temple pictures on the Barhut railings to the more elaborate structures of the extant temples of the Gupta period we have a natural development of considerable significance, vigorous and artistic but without any touch of sensuality. But in the 9th and 10th centuries, Hindu temple architecture in North India is overloaded with sculptures the beauty of which should not obscure the sensuality and often the obscenity of the themes portrayed. The Khajuraho and Orissa temples for all their magnificence testify to a degeneration of the Hindu mind, which sought to find in Vatsyayana the themes for their artistic expression. If this architecture stood by itself it might have been possible to argue it was merely a regrettable deviation from normalcy.

But the literature of the time provides even more convincing evidence of a general decadence. The direct, vigorous and humane poetry of Kalidasa reflects a contented and prosperous society. But the literature of the 9th and 10th centuries is gross and obscene to a degree and this is clearly no exception but a generally accepted fashion in all cultivated circles. The pornographic and obscene descriptions in great Kavyas written by poets of recognised respectability and virtue cannot be explained away as mere idiosyncrasies of taste. The great Vastu Pala, the Prime Minister to Vira Dhavala who built one of the marble temples of Abu and was in his day a most enlightened and charitable man, was also the author of *Nara Narayaniya* in which whole cantos are devoted to erotic descriptions. Kshemendra, the celebrated Kashmiri poet, is among the greatest educators of India, a populariser of the *Mahabharata, Brihadkatha* and even of the *Jataka* stories and yet he is also the author of *Samaya matrika*, the theme of which is the life of a prostitute. Again Damodara Gupta, a man of the highest standing in the society of the period, is known to us mainly as the author of *Kuttini matam*, a poem of extraordinary beauty, but the theme of which is prostitution. In the *Guhya Samaja* text, considered canonical and sacred by *tantrik* Buddhists, the Buddha is pictured in amorous dalliance with heavenly maidens; and the Hindu *tantrik* literature of the period contains many rituals of worship which can only be described as unnatural and obscene. In fact, examples can be multiplied to any extent to prove that the vigour and dynamism which marked Indian life to the end of the 8th century had given place to a degeneration which has no parallel in earlier Indian history. Scientific enquiry had come to a dead stop. Varaha Mihiras, Aryabhatas and Bhadanta Nagarjunas are memories of the past. As Al Beruni noted, the Hindu thinkers of the period were exclusive and arrogant and unwilling to learn from or to share their knowledge with others.

It is a major problem for Indian historians to study the question of this widespread decadence, which probably explains the surprisingly ineffective resistance to the Turki invaders from the North West. India, which was able to resist and throw back the armies of the great Khalifs, the greatest military power of the time, when they tried to penetrate into Gujerat and Rajasthan, lay prostrate before the adventurers from Central Asia. The vigour which enabled the Indian people successfully to resist the Sakas, the Huns and others who overturned empires elsewhere seems suddenly to have vanished in the 11th, 12th and 13th centuries.

I shall allude to one other problem which seems to me to require careful analysis and study. Muslim kingdoms and sultanates existed in Delhi continuously from the beginning of the 13th century to the downfall of the Moghuls in the 18th century. But leaving aside the Moghul Empire, which established a genuine administering state and exercised effective authority over North India for nearly 200 years, the extent of the authortiy of the Delhi sultans seems to me a subject worthy of the closest examination and study. Muslim historians have assumed on the basis of a Khalif's *fatwa* that the Delhi throne gave a legal right to the Empire of India. Following the Muslim writers, British historians also seem in the main to have accepted this doctrine. And yet the facts as we know them seem to go against such pretensions. Take the case of Kalinjar. Every great Muslim ruler claims to have conquered it anew, the last to do so being Humayun. When Babar invaded India, Gwalior, with its impregnable fortification, was in the hands of Tanwar rulers and he had in his turn to conquer it. Even in the Gangetic Valley which was directly under Delhi administration, there is some evidence to show that the authority of the Delhi sultans was not wholly effective.

Thus apart from Rajasthan and the vast area now included in Madhya Pradesh, Vindhya Pradesh and uplands like Chotanagpur, where Muslim rulers hardly penetrated and the authority of Islam was never effective, even in the territories under the direct rule of the Delhi sultans, the spirit of the Hindu people never seems to have broken. In fact, the most significant feature of the 14th and 15th centuries is the revival of Hinduism, to the study of which but little attention seems so far to have been devoted.

We have tended to identify the political life of mediæval India with the conquering expeditions of powerful monarchs and the chaos and confusion that reigned in the interval. The history of the Hindu people, who still constituted the vast majority and who reacted vigorously after a period of prostration, has been generally neglected.

There is another important fact relating to the study of Indian history to which I should like to allude. The emphasis on civilisation as the subject of historical study naturally enlarges the scope of Indian history, for Indian civilisation spread far and wide and created in South East Asia and in Central Asia Hinduised communities whose cultural and political achievements are legitimately a part of the wider Indian heritage. Much work has been done in this field. Now we have some idea of the expansion of Indian culture in Indonesia, Champa, Kambuja and Funan, of the history of Buddhism in China and of the great Hinduised civilisations which existed in Serindia. The opening up of this vast field of enquiry has been mainly the work of European scholars, Chavannes, Sylvain Levi, Coedes, Kern, Stutterheim, Foucher and others. Though the subject is of primary interest to us Indians, there has been but little Indian participation in this work. Dr. R. C. Mazumdar and Prof. Nilakanta Sastri have contributed to the interpretation of Indian achievement in South East Asia, but the basic studies have all been by European scholars. It is time that Indian scholars turned their attention to this subject and undertook research on their own. Much remains to be done not only to reconstruct the history of those areas but to establish their relationship with different parts of India, to relate the developments in Greater India to the political, economic and social conditions in the mother country, to evaluate the contribution of local peoples in the evolution of Javanese, Khmer and other civilisations and numerous other problems of a similar nature.

Also I am convinced that further and deeper study of Chinese history will help to explain many problems in India. Chinese historical material is vast. Much of it has not been explored for its bearing on India. Only in a superficial manner and as a bye-product of other studies has it been considered by Sinologists. The immense quantity of Indian literature, including a summarised version of the Ramayana belonging to the third century A.D., which Dr. Raghu Vira has brought back from China, after a preliminary visit, should open our eyes to the almost unlimited wealth which awaits any serious Indian student of Chinese history and civilisation. As at least from the third century B.C. India was known to the Chinese and further, as cultural relations between the two countries were close for over ten centuries, there is every reason to believe that a careful study of Chinese historical material will yield satisfactory results for the reconstruction of many periods of Indian history.

Indian history can only be understood in its proper setting. As the Italian scholar Luciano Petech has observed: "India and China, with Iran at their borders, are the pivots on which turns the cultural dynamism of the Far East. But this constant conflict and exchange of ideas and forms of civilisation took place for the most part on a ground where other political forces and other forms of life prevailed. The steppe belt to the north of China and India played a great part in the development of Asia as the medium through which all kinds of religious and artistic influence travelled, and as a political and military factor outrunning even the possibilities of the two major cultural powers. While it is true that the history of the civilisation of the Far East hinges on China and India, while it is true that the world has never seen another political organisation possessing the stability and continuity of the Chinese Empire, it is no less true that the steppes and the Gobi desert were factors of prime importance in determining the development of Asian history. This holds good not only for the purely political element provided by the great, but usually ephemeral, nomad empires which arose at irregular intervals in the steppes and the desert. But the peaceful and rich caravan cities of modern Sinkiang, made wealthy by the active trade in silk which nourished on that route down to the 8th century, cities that were politically quiescent and objects of the greed of both China and the nomads, acted as essential agencies for transmitting from one to the other of the three great cultural areas the germs of reciprocal fertilisation. And in this process they developed a composite and in some ways unique civilisation on their own.

"Without the steppe, without its nomad states and its caravan trade, China and India would have been limited to secondary currents of contact through South East Asia. In South East Asia, as I have already mentioned, an immense work of civilisation had been carried on for more than one thousand years; but it was this very work, arduous and difficult as it was, which led China and India to face each other there, since the earliest ages, as two opposite civilisations, each unchangeably firm in itself, with no possibility of fruitful exchanges. For Central Asia, on the contrary, I need only recall the part played by the caravan routes of the Tarim basin in the transmission eastward of Buddhism and its artistic elements which so deeply affected, by action and reaction, the evolution of Chinese society."

In fact the history of India, unless it is related to the developments in Central Asia, and in South East Asia would lose its full significance. Our vision of Indian history therefore requires to be widened, and the evolution and development of social and cultural forces in India have to be related to movements in these regions. This requires sustained research in the history of our neighbouring areas, for which we have so far been dependent on the work of European scholars. I would venture to appeal to the Government of India and to our universities for the establishment of chairs for Central Asian and South Eastern studies which are of primary concern to us in India. The Central Asian manuscripts in Delhi require to be carefully studied and edited. New expeditions have to be organised to carry on the work which was interrupted by the war; and the knowledge obtained has to be related to Indian developments. South East Asian studies are equally important for our history, and a great deal of fundamental work still remains to be done.

Also, generally, one cannot but deplore the neglect of Asian history by our universities. The key to many problems of Indian history lies in the movement of nomadic tribes from Central Asia, beginning perhaps with the Aryans themselves. The Sakas, the Yue Chis, the Huns, the Mongols and the Turks who at different times were pressing on the borders of India and who play so great a part in the history of north India represent vital movements of Asian history and have to be understood as such if our own growth and development have to be interpreted correctly; and yet so far as I know no serious effort has yet been made by any Indian university to make Asian history a principal subject of study, though we devote much of our time in familiarising ourselves with the European view of Western history.

The study of European history is undoubtedly important for us from the point of view both of methodology and modern developments. And yet it is a one-sided view of Europe that we are familiar with. Europeans writing their own history give an essentially distorted picture of world events. To read the standard historical writers in Europe one would think that, at all times, this peninsular projection of Asia was the centre of the world and the torch-bearer of civilisation; further that history is to be interpreted as a never-ending fight between Europe and Asia, beginning, in their view, with the Persian king's attack on Greece. One of the ironies of European historical thinking is this identification of Greece with the West. Actually much of Greek civilisation developed on the Asian coastal tract, in the borderland between Asia and Europe and many Asian civilisations, notably the Islamic, claim succession to the Greek. And yet by a bold stroke the European historians have annexed Greece to their own life, forgetting that Greece was not only practically unknown to Europe for nearly 1,000 years, and that the destruction of the Greek civilization of Byzantium was the supreme achievement of the West during the crusades. Indeed, if we have to study European history, as indeed we must, it should not be on the basis of the distorted picture presented to us by European scholars who see all later history as a homeric struggle between the East and the West. Lest I should be accused of exaggerating, I quote from a historian who takes pride in the claim that he does not approach history with any prejudice (Mr. H. A. L. Fisher). In discussing the Persian wars Mr. Fisher says: "For the next two hundred years the Persian menace was a governing factor in Greek politics. It was a rivalry between East and West, between despotism and liberty"; the West of course always standing for liberty and the East being sunk in despotism. His whole book may be said to be an interpretation of this text when it comes to relations with Asia.

Mr. Bernard Shaw says in one of his prefaces that when he read English history he gained the impression that the English were uniformly victorious; but that when he read French histories it was equally clear that the French led in all spheres. For us in India today to study European history from the point of view of Britain or even of Europe is to subject ourselves to subtle propaganda. What is important is to study European history objectively, to reinterpret European achievements from a world point of view and realise its significance for us. This is no doubt beyond our capacities today, but unless we devote our attention to it from now we shall be subjected to an intellectual dominance based on a distorted version of European history. In this connection I would invite attention to the work of American scholars on European history, which, though it still retains the inherited prejudices against Asia, takes a more objective view about Europe as a whole.

In conclusion, I would only make one appeal to Indian historians and that is not to lend themselves to the heresy of elevating regional glories as a result of their specialisation in certain periods or certain areas. Every region of India has contributed to the evolution of the Indian people; every group added to our common heritage. Every part of India has its heroic period and forgetting this the historians have often contributed to the false pride resulting from the glorified self-image of our different areas. This is a most dangerous development, which the historian has especially to guard against. We are entitled to take pride in the glories of

Magadha, or the achievement of the Palas or the Gurjara Pratiharas or the Cholas, Pallavas or Chalukyas or of Vijayanagar, the Moghuls or the Marathas, and yet our pride has to be that they have contributed to our common heritage. Believe me, there is no marked inequality in the intellectual or mental qualities of the different peoples of India and if at times some have been in the vanguard and others have lagged behind, in the general summing up, the contribution of each would seem to be significant. This is a point of view which I should like every student of history to bear in mind, for any other idea would inevitably lead to our ruin and disruption.

Indian Doctrines of Politics

IT IS MY first duty to thank the office-bearers of the Laski Institute for the honour they have done me by inviting me to deliver the inaugural address for the year. I am particularly happy to be able to do this because of the association of this body with the name of Harold Laski, for Laski is indeed one who is entitled to our gratitude in India and is in other ways also worthy of praise and commemoration. He is one of the germinal minds of England who have influenced Indian thinking for over a generation, for his personality, thought and teaching may be said to have dominated the progressive thinking of England in the inter-war period, influencing much of our own thinking in politics. It is not necessary for me to discuss here Laski's contribution to the political thought of the century. He was not in any sense a schematic thinker, with a perfected system of political doctrines or a new school of political philosophy. In fact the strands of many schools of thought could be traced in his teachings. A socialist who was in a general sense a Marxian thinker, he was also an inheritor to the radical thought of 19th century England, an interpreter of Bodin's doctrine of sovereignty and at the same time a thinker who emphasised the limitations to the theory of undivided sovereignty which the growth of group-organisation had imposed on the modern state. It could, therefore, be said that diverse trends of political thinking converged on him, sometimes giving an impression of contradiction in the views which he held at different times. This was perhaps

Address to the Laski Institute of Political Science, Ahmedabad, 1955.

inevitable in the circumstances of the world in which men of his generation lived. In the formative years of Laski's life, the sunset glow of Victorian radicalism still illumined the world. The first Great War saw the end of that world. In the period between the two wars, when the main part of his activity lay, the world was a cockpit of conflicting values, having lost the faith in the liberal state, and with many rival doctrines claiming allegiance. The October Revolution in Russia had established a dictatorship of the proletariat and the Marxian doctrine had become the philosophy in office in the Soviet Union. The rise of the Labour Party to power in England had created new problems which were of special interest to the theorist of politics. The structure of the British Empire underwent a change by the Statute of Westminster which would have scandalised the doctrinaires of sovereignty of an earlier period. More than half of Europe had fallen under the spell of the leadership doctrine, with Duces, Führers and Caudillos posturing as new Caesars and imposing on their peoples new theories of social reaction. In fact the changes in ideas were so rapid that only a rigid and wooden mind, insensitive to its own surroundings, could have maintained a consistency of opinion during this period.

If the claim of Laski to greatness did not lie in any special contribution to the theory of politics, in what did it lie? In my opinion it lay in something much more important—a truly critical and unprejudiced spirit which was able to analyse, expound and illuminate the many problems with which the world of his time was confronted. It is this critical spirit which made him a torch-bearer in his time and gave him an influence over the mind of people—especially young people—which men of greater originality and deeper vision envied. His spirit is of great value to us in India today and I am glad to be associated with you all in honouring him.

Laski spent a lifetime lecturing and writing on political science: on political institutions, theories and practices. The melancholy fact about India today is that political science is the most neglected course of study in our universities, one on which there has been little or no original contribution made by our thinkers. The textbooks which are taught in our universities and the doctrines which are expounded by our teachers and studied by our students are so unrelated to our social order, and are generally speaking so foreign to our experience that I have often wondered whether, as at present constituted, these studies serve any purpose at all. To study Aristotle, Bodin, Hobbes, Rousseau, Green and others may be an intellectual discipline; to be familiar with their views may be a part of liberal education; to be concerned with such imprecise terms as democracy, dictatorship, will of the people and social contract, may not be less useful than being engaged in perpetual discussions on metaphysical problems, but no one could pretend that they touch the hard core of power in society.

If our university teaching has been barren on this vital subject it is an equally regrettable fact that there has been no systematic thinking in modern India outside academic life on the foundations of politics. Most of the great political thinkers of the West, Hobbes, Locke, Rousseau, Marx and the rest were not connected with any centres of learning. In India our leaders of thought have never considered it worth while to examine the relation of the individual to the state. No political leader among us has tried to formulate any theory of social order, enquire into the principles on which we have reared our political institutions, examine the validity of the many assumptions of our public life. Indeed this is a strange and melancholy situation.

And yet, when we think about it, India is one of the few countries in which political science was in the past studied as an independent subject. *Artha Sastra* was one of the orthodox courses of study which never really died out in India till the 16th century, for in the first quarter of that century we have Krishna Deva Raya of Vijayanagar writing a treatise of considerable interest on the subject. A Malayalam commentary on Kautilya discovered a few years ago, on which Ganapathi Sastri based his own commentary, displays deep interest in the problems of political science and treats many unfamiliar questions with originality and acumen. In fact a history of Hindu political science from Kautilya to Krishna Deva Raya would show an originality and variety of thought as remarkable as the history of political thought anywhere, while the vast literature of our *Dharmasastras* and *Nibandhas* would provide a study of social development, as reflected in laws and legal institutions, which constitute a no less important aspect of political science. And yet for the last half a century we have been content to equate political theories with what Aristotle wrote or what Rousseau preached. The development of independent political thinking related to our own social order and institutional structure is the basic need of India today. No doubt this can be done independently of what has been thought or written in the past in India, but it cannot be done satisfactorily, for what our Acharyas taught in the past related to our own conditions and are, therefore, very much with us, a part of our intellectual inheritance even if we are not aware of it. The *Mahabharata*, that encyclopaedia of Indian thinking, which has been the one instrument of the education of the Indian mind, and to which, in spite of all our familiarity with Western literature and thought, we still return for the solution of our problems, is the central text of our political science also. Many different schools of political science are incorporated in the *Santi Parvam*.

What is political science? I might briefly describe it as dealing with three questions: the why and wherefore of the state, the nature of the state, the source of its authority, its institutions, etc. and the relation of the individual to the state. All other questions can be related to these three. Indian political thinkers tried to go to the root of these problems, and the discussions on these topics in the *Mahabharata* if rendered in modern phraseology would be as striking today as the treatises of the most modern Western political philosophers.

This is how the first question, the why and wherefore of the state, is formulated in the *Mahabharata:* "Why does one man rule over persons of great intelligence and valour although he has the same physical organs and mental attributes, is subject to the same changes of birth and death and is equal in all respects to others?" This is the question that Yudhisthira asks of Bhishma. Though formulated in terms of kingship, the problem is the same in regard to the state—the impersonal sovereign who claims our allegiance. The answer of Bhishma is indeed interesting: "In the beginning there was neither state nor monarch; neither law nor the criminal."

Naiva Rājyam na Rāja sin na ca dando na dandika.

The result in due course was that men were sunk in greed, wealth and self-indulgence: in the law of the jungle, which is described picturesquely as *Matsya Nyaya*—the rule of the fish, the big ones eating up the smaller. It was thus to ensure safety and to secure social order that the state was created. This doctrine, it will be seen, is similar to what Hobbes teaches. According to Hobbes, "The final cause, end and design of men in the introduction of that restraint on themselves (in which we see them live in commonwealths) is the foresight of their own preservation and of a more contented life thereby; that is to say, of getting themselves out from the miserable condition of war which is necessarily consequent to the natural passions of man when there is no visible power to keep them in awe and tie them by fear of punishment." Thus, it is to avoid the anarchy resulting from *Matsya Nyaya* that the state is established. Hobbes' description of what he calls the state of war prevailing under the natural condition of man is strikingly similar to the description in the *Mahabharata* of the anarchy preceding the establishment of the state. Says Hobbes: "Hereby it is manifest that during the time that men live without a common power to keep them all in awe they are in that condition which is called war and such a war as is of every man against every man, for war consisteth not in battle only or the act of fighting but in a tract of time wherein the will to contend by battle is known. . . . The nature of war consisteth not in actual fighting but in the known disposition thereto. . . .

"Whatever therefore is consequent to a time of war where

every man is enemy to every man, the same is consequent to the time wherein men live without other security than that their own strength and their own invention shall furnish them with all. In such a condition there is no place for industry, because the fruit thereof is uncertain and consequently no culture of the earth; no navigation nor use of the commodities that may be imported by sea; no account of time; no arts; no letters; no society and which is worst of all, continual fear and the danger of violent death and the life of man solitary, poor, nasty, brutish and short."

This may be compared with Bhishma's description of the conditions of life before the state is established.

Arājakesu Rāstrēsu na dharmo Vyavastisthate
Parasparam ca khādante sarvadā dhigarājakam

Where a non-state condition exists Dharma will not exist and men will eat (destroy) each other. Quoting Brihaspati, he then gives the following graphic description of what Hobbes describes as the state of war:

"The strong will abduct the wives of the weak
There will be no feeling that this is mine
The rules of morality will not be followed
The wicked will take away by force (others') carriages, clothes, ornaments, etc.
People will kill their own parents, old men, teachers, guests and . . . .
Good men will be oppressed and the wicked will be strong
The rich will live in fear of life and of being imprisoned
Friendship will not be recognised
There will be no ploughing, no agriculture, no trade."

Thus Bhishma establishes the doctrine which is basic to all Hindu thought on politics, that the state is the outcome of the desire of man for security, for a social order in which he can live in peace and enjoy the fruits of his own labour and not be subjected to *Matsya Nyaya*. It may be noted that the father of modern European political thinking, Nicolo Machiavelli, in his discourse on Livy says: "At first men lived like brutes, then they thought of choosing a chief for their better protection."

It is on this point that the ancient Hindu thinkers were at variance with the Aristotelian view, which postulated that "the state is a creation of nature and that man is by nature a political animal"; that is man cannot be conceived outside the state, the condition of anarchy previous to the establishment of the state is altogether inconceivable; that "the state is prior to the family and the individual since the whole is of necessity prior to the part". Further Aristotle affirmed that as the state or the political community is "the highest of all and embraces all the rest" it aims at the "highest good". Of course anthropology was an unknown subject in the time of Aristotle and the idea of the state being logically at least antecedent to man, and being a creation of nature need not, therefore, be taken too literally. But it is necessary to emphasise that many orthodox schools of political thought in the West find in this view a justification for their exaltation of the state as being something superior to man, as a natural institution embodying the principles of highest good.

A further point of difference between the Hindu and the Greek approach to political thought may be emphasised here. Yudhisthira, as we noticed, asked Bhishma why one man should have authority over others since all are equal. It is the natural equality of man and the contradiction of his having to obey others that raises the problem in Yudhisthira's mind. But the approach of Aristotle is different. He starts with the assumption: "that some should rule and others be ruled is not only necessary but expedient; from the hour of birth, some are marked out for subjection, others for rule." Greek political thought, contrary to the Hindu view on politics, proceeds on an assumption of natural inequality.

Now we may turn to the second question—the nature of the state, its institutions and qualities. That no state can exist without coercive power will not today be denied. That the state represents force both externally and internally is an obvious fact. The dualism between Dharma and Artha which is never wholly absent in Hindu thought but which comes out most prominently in that the science of politics is known as Artha Sastra, enables Hindu thinkers to evolve a purely secular theory of state of which the sole basis is power. Bhishma goes even further and proclaims the doctrine that even a usurper, as he upholds social order and is the embodiment of power, should be obeyed. *Indrāya sa pranamatē namatē yo baliyasē*: and the great Ausanis tradition—always more radical than the orthodox—represented by Sukraniti goes to the extent of saying that the sovereign is only respected for his power.

It is in their analysis of the quality of the state and its functions that the Hindu thinkers on politics show the greatest originality. The basic doctrine in this connection is the conception of the state as the maker of the epoch which Bhishma puts pithily in the phrase, *Rāja Kālasya Kāranam.* How universally accepted this view was may be seen from the fact that Manu, Narada, Gautama and other writers on Smriti elaborate and emphasise the point. For example, it is stated in Manu that the various ways in which a sovereign behaves constitutes the *Kṛta, Trēta, Dwāpara* and *Kali* ages—periods of time based on quality. The same idea is repeated by other Smriti writers (Narada XVIII—20.33, Gautama VIII—I—11). In the *Mahabharata* it is stated explicitly:

Kālo va kāranam rājno
Rāja va kāla kāranam
Iti tē samsayam mā bhūt
Rāja kālasya kāranam

Now what is meant by saying that the sovereign is the maker of the age? The characteristics of the age, whether they be progressive, prosperous, based on social justice, reactionary, repressive or socially stagnant are the results of the sovereign's action. How true this is we can see from our experience. We see before our eyes a mighty transformation taking place, a transformation which has the undoubted characteristic of the change of an age. Our social life is being remoulded, economic justice is being brought about, there is a great striving for prosperity. Everywhere we notice a basic change. This is being brought about by the sovereign state through its initiative and mainly under its direction. The state is here seen in its capacity as *Kālasya kāranam,* the maker of the age. That this is not a strained interpretation but what was meant by the early teachers is made clear by Bhishma's statement:

Kritam trēta dwāparcca
Kalicca Bharatarshabha
Rāja vrittani sarvāni
Rājaiva yugam uchyatē

All the ages, in their different qualities, are what the sovereign makes of them. It is the sovereign itself who should be spoken of as the age. The author of *Sukra niti sara* emphasises this factor further. After pointing out that the true conception of the age is according to the deeds and activities of men, he states that "the sovereign is the cause of the setting on foot of customs and usages (social legislation) and movements and hence is the cause and maker of time. If the age or time were the cause, there could be no virtue in the actors."

From all this it follows that the conception of the state in India was not one based on *laissez faire* or the mere maintenance of law and order, but one of direct activity to further progress.

The institutional study of the state has been a feature of Indian political thinking from the earliest times. While the doctrines of the state in the West was one of estates, based on class, as was but natural where feudal ideas prevailed, in India the state was defined as having seven *prakritis* or essential institutional features. The state, says Kautilya, is an organisation of seven limbs, the sovereign, the officialdom, the territory, the fort (defensive measures), the treasury (sound finances), military establishments and international relations. Stated briefly the Hindu state involves a defined territory, a swamin or a supreme head, an organisation of executive government, military power, foreign policy, and adequate financial resources. Kautilya when he describes *Rājā rajyam iti prakriti samksepah* does not mean that the Ruler and the state are one, but that sovereignty involves all this, and a state without any of the sapta prakritis is not a fully sovereign state.

A major difference between the Western and Indian conceptions of the state is in reference to administration. In Western Europe the administering state came into existence only with Colbert. The idea that administration was one of the essential functions of the state and therefore deserved to be studied as a part of political science does not appear to have been realised by writers on political science till the second half of the 19th century. From Aristotle to Austin, none of the writers devotes any attention to the question of administrative machinery. Bagehot who wrote a classical treatise on the British Constitution does not allude to the civil services of England, and even Dicey, a later writer who exercised great influence on English thinking, shows no realisation of the importance of the administrative machinery as one of the major organs of the state. The Indian point of view was different at all times. From the very beginning the main function of the state in India was administration. As is well known, in Kautilya's *Artha Sastra* we have not merely a treatise on politics but a handbook of administration. The number and variety of departments whose functions Kautilya describes show that the conception of the state always included economic and public works activity, industry, irrigation, maintenance of roads, superintendence and encouragement of commerce, care of forests, etc. In fact the state described by Kautilya was all-embracing in its activity unlike the feudal states of Europe. Later writers equally recognise and emphasise administration as an essential feature of state organisation.

Another special feature of Hindu political thinking is the doctrine of the three saktis: mantra sakti, prabhu sakti and utsahā sakti as the governing principles of the state. Mantra sakti is the power of good counsel—of free discussion and careful deliberation. Special emphasis is laid on the necessity of free discussion, for good counsel on which the sovereign has to depend can only come from unfettered deliberation, prabhu sakti is the strength derived from sound finances and internal stability, and utsaha sakti is the power derived from initiative and sustained action. The purpose of higher state policy was said to combine these three. Kautilya includes in the definition of mantra five elements: deliberation on the methods of initiating a policy, determination of the instruments of policy and the ways and means for carrying out policy, consideration of suitable time, place, etc., consideration of possible difficulties and obstacles and successful termination. With the best mantra sakti a state cannot prosper unless it has prabhu sakti—strength derived from the general soundness of finance, the stability of administration and prosperity of the people. And finally, even with both of these, a state cannot achieve success unless there is sustained action based on sound initiative.

This emphasis on initiative is particularly interesting because there is a continuous insistence that in matters connected with the state it is human endeavour alone that counts. In a striking passage Bhishma declares:

> Sādharanam dwayam hi etad
> Daivam uthānam ēva ca
> Paurusham hi param many
> Daivam niccittyam ūhyate

Of these two, Fate and human endeavour, the latter is the one to be depended upon, for the former is only inferential. The state relates to activity in this world and therefore uthānam or human endeavour should be the sure foundation of all state activity.

Now we may consider the last basic question we formulated, the relation of the individual to the state in Indian political thinking. We have already noticed that the state in India was all-embracing in its activity. There was no sphere except that of Dharma which was excluded from its view. As an administering state it touched the life of every individual. Beyond the protection that Dharma afforded to him, the individual had no rights against the state. The state was omnipotent, it had no "estates" to limit its activity or to resist its fiats. The protection that Dharma afforded was to the community in general and not to the individual. The question of civil, political and religious rights, therefore, was not the subject of speculation and this was the main weakness of Hindu political thought. The assumption in Yudhisthira's question about contradiction betwen human equality and the superiority of the sovereign becomes limited to the difference between an individual and the person of the ruler for between an individual and a state, such as Kautilya describes, the problem does not arise, because the control of the individual has become the main function of the administering state. No doubt the theorists talk of Praja hitam—the welfare of the people—as being the sole object of the sovereign, but such statements have no relation to the rights of the individual.

I shall speak only about one more aspect of the Hindu conception of state and that is the doctrine of justice. Enforcement of justice was conceived of as part of the duty of affording protection, of rakshana, of saving the people from the matsya nyaya, of the big fish eating the small ones. But what was the Hindu conception of justice? The question was formulated thus in the *Mahabharata:* "What is justice? What is its nature, what is its form, what is its essence? How again does it remain vigilant and maintain itself among the people? How does it keep awake and continuously evolve? Where does it reside, what are its ways?" The answer to these questions gives the Hindu view of justice in relation to the state. Danda is so called in order that the righteousness of the sovereign who is wide awake may not suffer extinction. Danda is (an aspect of) Vishnu, the protector. It is the permanent form of Divinity on earth. The daughter of God is known (synonymously) by the name of Lakshmi, Niti (moral laws), Saraswati and Danda Niti. Two points are emphasised here: first that justice is what binds society together and is the great protective principle, and secondly that economic prosperity, moral welfare and cultural advancement are dependent on justice. Manu as a law-giver is equally emphatic. "Justice", he says, "keeps awake while all are asleep. The wise men know Danda to be Dharma. The people are made happy only by the proper administration of justice."

We have now briefly touched on the main features of the Indian conception of the state; its origin, its functions and the institutions through which it operates. There is one further idea which governs ancient Indian thinking in this matter. It is considered axiomatic, not requiring any arguments to establish it. It is that as an organ of Dharma the state is subordinate to it. It is beyond the competence of the state to alter Dharma and this operated as an effective limitation on what would otherwise have been a totalitarian conception. The right of the people to revolt against a sovereign who does not follow Dharma is expressly laid down. If the sovereign be an enemy of Dharma then the people should desert him as causing the ruin of the state, says Sukra. In the *Mahabharata* it is laid down that a king who does not afford protection according to Dharma "should be slain by his combined subjects like a mad dog afflicted with rabies". The supremacy of Dharma was an assumption of Indian political thought which operated to limit the omnipotence of the state.

Indian political thought included many different schools. As it was a subject which was widely studied, there arose different theories and doctrines, some conservative, some radical and some following a middle path. Three main schools, apart from the eclectic and practical school of Kautilya, could be traced. In the *Mahabharata* itself Bhishma quotes the views of the Brihaspati and Ausanas schools, the first supposed to emanate from the guru of the Devas and the other from the guru of the Danavas. Apart from what is contained in the *Mahabharata* we have the Ausanas tradition embodied in the *Sukra niti sara*, a handbook summarising an authoritative treatise belonging to this school. Sukra is the most radical of our political thinkers, for he does not hesitate even to say that the sovereign is but a salaried servant of the people

(Chapter 1, sloka 375). He further enjoins that a sovereign "however wise, however proficient in all the sciences and a master of statecraft should never by himself study political interests without proper discussion with his ministers. A wise ruler should ever abide by the well-thought-out decisions of councillors, officers and members of his sabha. The monarch who follows his own will is the cause of miseries, soon gets estranged from his kingdom and alienated from the people." The Brihaspati tradition may be said to be represented by the *Kamandaka niti sara.*

Apart from these essentially doctrinal writings we have also an outstanding contribution to the science of politics in Kautilya's *Artha Sastra.* The historian Acton in speaking of Machiavelli says: "The first paramount fact with which modern history begins is that the state is above right and wrong. While it pursues its own objects, acquires power, increases territory, promotes prosperity, raises renown or gratifies the pride of the nation, it is not to be prevented or censured because it employs the basest of crimes, taking of human life by war, etc." This description is applicable even to a greater extent to Kautilya. But Kautilya was much more than the theorist of the amoral state. His conception of the state was far beyond the limited imagination of Machiavelli, for he thought of the state as an organisation which took within the range of its interests every sphere of human activity—in fact it was the prototype of the modern omnipotent administering state.

I trust I have said sufficient to show that India has inherited a tradition in political thought which is at least as original as anything in the West, which discusses freely, frankly and with deep insight all the fundamental problems relating to political communities and further emphasises the administrative and economic functions of a state in a manner generally unknown to European writers before the 19th century. And yet today this study is neglected in our schools. We are content to repeat what Western writers have said in regard to their societies, the historical conditions under which they developed, without understanding our own conditions and the traditions which are still powerful in our country. Current Indian political thinking will not cease to be a pale reflection of Western ideas until we try to understand Indian social and political institutions in terms of Indian thinking. It is in this connection that I feel gratified that societies like yours should address themselves to the science of politics, for the great man whose name is associated with this institution was one who brought a powerful and critical mind to bear not merely on the problems of the day but also on the thought of others. He was always ready to attack the realities of contemporary politics, while he analysed and expounded what he considered valid in the doctrines of the theorists who had gone before. That is what we should also do. We should develop a living and virile school of political thought, directly related to the conditions of our country. This should be your main function: to study deeply but with a critical mind the political thought developed in India in relation to such thinking elsewhere and particularly in relation to the present conditions of our own political community.

Sanskrit in Modern India

I FEEL particularly honoured to have been invited to inaugurate this session of the All-India Sanskrit Parishad, Lucknow. I have no claims to scholarship in Sanskrit. My knowledge of Sanskrit and its literature is that of a layman fairly familiar with the classics of the language. I can, however, claim a life-long devotion not merely to the literature enshrined in the language but to the civilisation that it represents and embodies. Therefore, I look upon your invitation as a recognition of the importance of a layman's approach to the position of Sanskrit in our life.

I take it that this is an institution whose object is to encourage the cultivation of Sanskrit, to emphasise its importance to our national life, to popularise its study and generally to uphold the claims of Sanskrit as the common source of our inspiration before the general public. Stated in those broad terms, few will take objection to it. But it is well to examine the point more closely. What do the promoters of this institution seek to achieve? Surely, not to make the study of Sanskrit a universal and compulsory feature of our education, for it is an impossible object to achieve. Equally, it could not be to obtain employment or make the material benefits of Sanskrit education more alluring or secure the worldly advancement of Sanskrit scholars; for, though both may be desirable, it is impossible to see how, in our present-day world, higher knowledge in a classical language can add

Inaugural Address at the Akhil Bharatiya Sanskrit Parishad, Lucknow, 1954.

to the market value of an individual. I assume also that the Parishad does not concern itself with research or critical editions or publications of old texts, all of which are necessary but within the proper sphere of specialised institutions. This Parishad and other institutions of a similar character have, to my mind, the more important function of keeping alive those great qualities of form and beauty, those great treasures of wisdom, knowledge and thought, those imperishable traditions of culture and civilisation which belong to India as a whole. For, Sanskrit is truly our most precious national inheritance, a fact to which I shall have occasion to revert later. What this institution represents is the selfless enthusiasm of its promoters for a noble and worthy cause.

I am not unaware of the apprehensions felt in some quarters that the study of Sanskrit is an encouragement to reaction, that those who advocate it are trying to turn the mind of India backward to the past, that it is an invitation to the mind of youth to accept discarded social theories. This apprehension is altogether unwarranted. It is no doubt true that some of those who pass as Pandits and Shastris often seem to accept as authoritative anything that is embodied in a classical text and argue against even the most necessary reforms on the basis of some Smriti whose only importance arises from its being clothed in Sanskrit; that there is often a tendency on the part of those who have spent their time in studying old texts to consider that all arguments are concluded when they have found an apt quotation. It is no doubt equally true that conservative minds often turn to the authorities in Sanskrit to buttress their opinion. But I may venture to point out that this is nothing special to Sanskrit. I could quote equally authoritative texts from English or French to justify reaction. It is also undeniable that authoritative texts can be found in Sanskrit to justify the more progressive views. One point, however, is worth emphasising. Merely because a thought is expressed in Sanskrit, it does not achieve validity or attain sacredness. In the case of a language like Sanskrit which has been actively cultivated for over 4000 years, there are bound to be many things which are out-of-date, some which are patently wrong, others which are merely the reflections of a particular stage of society. For example, it is no use considering as valid the anatomy which is taught in ancient Sanskrit books when it is demonstrably absurd, or proclaiming *Charaka Samhita* to be the last word in Surgery merely because they are in Sanskrit. Similar is the case with regard to the *Smritis.* No one who has read *Manava Dharma Shastra* will presume to deny that it is a work of the greatest significance in the world of law, but to claim that because it is written in Sanskrit by a great Rishi it is authoritative in the circumstances of today would be the height of foolishness. Sanskrit scholars brought up entirely in the traditional knowledge have not been wholly free from this fault and it is this attitude that has given rise to the apprehension that to make the study of Sanskrit popular would be to encourage reaction.

On the other hand, it can be clearly demonstrated that all great reforms which have changed the face of India have originated from those who had studied Sanskrit deeply. It is unnecessary to speak of Swami Dayanand. But Ram Mohan Roy, the father of progressive thinking in India, Vivekanand who fought so energetically for social uplift, and Aurobindo who gave a new life to ancient teachings, to mention only a few, were all men who had drunk deep in the life-giving water of *Girvani.*

Also, we are inclined to forget that Sanskrit is not exclusively the possession of the Hindus. True, the Hindus have their sacred books in Sanskrit but let us not forget that the canonical texts of Mahayana are also in Sanskrit and that equally it is the sacred language of the Jains. It is a narrow and altogether erroneous view which limits Sanskrit to Hinduism, for who is there who would give up *Buddha Charita* and *Saundarananda* of Ashwaghosha, *Nagananda* of Shri Harsha, the *Bodhisattvavadana Kalpa Lata* of Kshemendra, to mention only a few Buddhist classics, or the great masterpieces of Hemachandra Suri when counting the wealth of Sanskrit literature. I leave aside the philosophic, religious and logical treatises of the Mahayanists and the Jains which constitute in themselves an immense and most valuable literature. The point I desire to emphasise is that Sanskrit is not the monopoly of the Hindus, but that its literature, and the vast realms of thought it covers, embody the whole mind of India; its positivism, no less than its mystical leanings; its spirit of enquiry and doubt, no less than its dogmatism; its yearning for material prosperity, no less than its striving for spiritual deliverance. If in the past our teachings of Sanskrit, owing to certain traditional inhibitions, concentrated only on orthodoxy, it is not the fault of Sanskrit but of the system of education inherited by us.

The study of Sanskrit is not a luxury and should not be looked upon as such. When we consider that the ideas, the literary forms and even the themes of the literature of our great regional languages are predominantly derived from Sanskrit; that for the proper use of a large percentage of words, even in Dravidian languages, an understanding of Sanskrit is necessary; that the great classics of India, not only the *Ramayana* and the *Mahabharata,* but the masterpieces from which everyone in India draws his inspiration, from the simple *Panchatantra* to *Shakuntala*, are in Sanskrit, and it is on their translations and their vulgarisations that our minds are fed and nourished from childhood, it will, I am sure, be conceded that a knowledge of Sanskrit, however imperfect, is a necessity and not a luxury. That it is so to the literary man, to the thinker and to the scholar would seem to be axiomatic. It may be asked why it should be so for the politician, for the man of affairs, for anyone who claims to be educated. The answer is that apart from Sanskrit being our greatest single national inheritance, the roots of our national behaviour, the pattern of our thought and the source of all our ideas being embedded in Sanskrit, a familiarity with it is necessary for anyone who claims to be a true Indian.

I do not say that a study of Panini's *Ashtadhyayi* or Patanjali's *Bhashya* is necessary for everyone. Indeed I deprecate greatly the emphasis on grammar which has been the ruin of Sanskrit studies. Many of you will remember the story of Gunadhya's *Brihat Katha* quoted in Somadeva's

Kathasaritsagara, how a new grammar, the *Katantra,* had to be composed in order to make the study of Sanskrit easy for the King. Whether the story is true or not, it deals with an issue which is a very major one even today. To equate knowledge of Sanskrit with *Vyutpatti* or the creation or formation of words from roots, according to the rules laid down by Panini is to attach undue importance to linguistics, and to forget the substance for the form. Many of us write and speak freely in English, read the great literature of that language, but how few of us know the *Vyutpatti* of a single word, or are familiar with the works of the great English grammarians. A knowledge of the essentials of grammar is necessary to understand any language well, but the idea that seems to be exclusively prevalent in the world of Sanskrit scholarship that no one can be said to know Sanskrit unless he has mastered the intricacies of Sanskrit grammar seems to me exceptionally puerile. Indeed, if you are interested in popularising Sanskrit as a language of culture, the essential thing to do is to take it out of the hands of grammarians and teach it as we teach other languages, by giving the student the necessary vocabulary and minimum grammatical apparatus to enable him to understand the classics. It is, of course, necessary for those whose aim is scholarship or who desire to write in Sanskrit or for those who have to teach it to study it in the hard way of mastering the intricacies of grammar. But for the layman who, let us say, desires to read the works of Kalidasa in the original, or to understand Shankara's commentary on the *Gita* such a knowledge of grammar I consider to be unimportant exactly in the same way as a knowledge of Skeat's Grammar is not necessary for a person desiring to read the plays of Shakespeare, or to follow the metaphysics of Berkeley. This is a subject to which I would venture to invite your attention—the introduction of a course of what may be called Basic Sanskrit with a minimum of, and, where possible, regular grammatical rules and a vocabulary of commonly used words.

Earlier, I said that Sanskrit is the one common national inheritance of India. The South and the North, the West and the East have equally contributed to it. No part of India can claim it as its exclusive possession. When we talk of our national genius being unity in diversity, of the fundamental oneness of the Indian mind, etc., what we really mean is the dominance of Sanskrit which over-rides the regional differences and linguistic peculiarities and achieves a true national character in our thought and emotions and even gives form and shape to the languages.) So far as I know there has never been an instance in world history when a language which was but the speech of an invading few was able to establish its unchallenged authority over a whole sub-continent and be its permanently unifying factor for over two thousand years. (Sanskrit is India's one national language and whatever position Hindi may achieve as Vyavahara Bhasha of the common languages of the future, the unity of India will collapse if it ceases to be related to Sanskrit or breaks away from the Sanskritic tradition. Sanskrit alone has that pre-eminence, which Hindi could never claim, over the great regional languages, enabling her to maintain and uphold in every region of India the supreme claim of Indian unity. It may indeed be said that one who knows Sanskrit is a better Indian for he is in a position to appreciate what every part of India has contributed to it. With Vyasa he could roam about in the forests and pilgrimage centres of the whole country; with Valmiki he could visit Lanka; with Kalidasa see the glories of Ujjain, walk in the Himalayan valleys, or follow the cloud from Ramagiri to Kailash; with Bhartrihari contemplate on the vanities of the world; with the merchants of Somadeva travel to Dwipantaras and even to Kanakapuri; with Sudraka live the life of a gay nagarika. Through Sanskrit we get something added to us from every part of India. Kalhana makes us live with the Kings of Kashmir. With Jona Raja we share in the glory of Prithwiraja. We take from Jayadeva some of his ecstasy, from Hemachandra Suri his gift of being able to illumine almost anything. With Queen Gangadevi of Vijayanagar we march on Madurai. With Bhavabhuti we sport on the Godavari. With Dandin we are at the Pallava court at Kanchi. With Narayana Bhatta we are in Kerala. With Jagannatha Pandita we taste a little of the magnificence of Shah Jahan.

A language which opens its wide gates to so extensive a realm; which reflects the thoughts, the emotions and the yearnings of 4000 years; whose diction is rich and mellifluous beyond compare, and is charged with feeling and sensibility, a language which has been used to express the highest metaphysical thoughts as well as the most beautiful poetry, is an inheritance so precious and so unique that every Indian claiming to be educated must have some knowledge of it. But in our veneration for Sanskrit and in our pride in its glories we should not overlook the fact that there are also wide gaps in that literature. Sanskrit represents a great civilisation in all its strength and weaknesses, in its growth and in its decay. Where that civilisation was weak, as in historical literature, or in social sciences, or where its growth was arrested as in mathematics and physical sciences, Sanskrit also reflected these tendencies. What is important today is that we should try and modernise the content of Sanskrit: we must ensure that anatomy does not cease with works written in the fourth century, that astronomy does not end with Varahamihira and Bhaskara, that medicine does not end with *Astangahridaya.* In the field of history and social sciences, where Sanskrit is singularly barren, I do not see why it should not be possible to enrich the language by rendering into it classics from modern languages as are of special importance to us. A good history of India in Sanskrit would, in my opinion, be a major contribution while a study of *Niti shastra* in terms of modern thinking, and without keeping to the mould of Kautilya, Shukra or Kamandaka, may indeed be of the highest value in explaining modern conceptions to those accustomed to think in old terms.

Nor is it sufficient to limit the modernisation of Sanskrit to these unfamiliar subjects. As a great world language I consider it essential that Sanskrit should possess a literature of translations from the classics of the world. Dante's *Divine Comedy*, Goethe's *Faust*, the masterpieces of Greek tragedy, some of the plays of Shakespeare and other great works which may legitimately be claimed as the inheritance of the civilised world should surely be rendered into Sanskrit. Not long ago I came across some plays written in elegant Sanskrit prose on modern themes by a South Indian writer. I have also had occasion to read a translation of Omar Khayyam's *Rubaiyat* in Sanskrit. In fact the amount of original work of more than ordinary merit that is being done in Sanskrit is astonishing. But generally speaking they keep to old forms and are content to be imitative and to echo the sentiments of the great masters. What I would venture to suggest is that the available scholarship should be used to provide Sanskrit with a basis of modernisation, to import into it, and naturalise in the language, new literary forms like modern fiction and short stories, new directions in poetry, not necessarily in conformity with the doctrines of Alankarikas, to open up new areas like history, biography and short essays. Thus would Sanskrit become once again a language of living culture.

There is one other aspect which I would emphasise in this connection. The literature of the Reformation of Hinduism, unlike that of earlier periods, has been, with two notable exceptions—the *Satyartha Prakash* of Swami Dayanand, and *Gita Rahasya* of Tilak—in English. From Ram Mohan to Aurobindo and Radhakrishnan, the new interpretations of Indian thought, whether they be commentaries on the *Gita* or the *Upanishads* or independent writings like the *Life Divine* of Aurobindo, have found in English a suitable medium of expression. That was perhaps inevitable in view of the fact that through English alone was it possible to reach every corner of India. But now, when it is clear that in course of time English will lose its pre-eminence as the language of thought, what guarantee is there that the gains of our new learning will be consolidated, preserved and indeed enlarged unless they are rendered into Sanskrit and thereby enabled to achieve a position of orthodoxy for the future? It is my considered opinion that one of the main duties of the Sanskrit scholars of this generation is to incorporate into our permanent national language, which is undeniably Sanskrit, the achievements of the Indian mind during the last hundred years.

This is possible only if there is a centre of learning. A Samskrita Vishwa Vidyalaya which will devote itself to the modernisation of Sanskrit and its utilisation for the purposes of higher learning is to my mind essential if the unity of Indian culture is to be preserved. This will also help to popularise the national language, Hindi, as the Constitution provides that it should be based primarily on Sanskrit, and *ex hypothesi,* unless Sanskrit itself becomes flexible and modernised, Hindi will not be enriched in its modern forms by association with Sanskrit. Clearly, Sanskrit and Hindi have to move forward hand in hand and I earnestly hope that Sanskrit scholars everywhere will take up with enthusiasm the establishment of one or more universities to impart modern humanistic education through Sanskrit.

If we look back on our three thousand years of known history, one thing will stand out clearly. At all periods of great national achievements there has been a revival of Sanskrit as an index to the virility of Indian nationhood. It was in the period of Maurya greatness that many of the great works of Sanskrit came to be written. It was the Gupta period that witnessed the recensions of the epics and the Puranas and the great efflorescence of classical Sanskrit poetry. In the period of the Kanauj Empire flourished Harsha himself, Bana, Mayura and other poets. The Parmara Empire of Bhoja has become a legend in literature. When northern India passed under Muslim rule, Gujerat which flourished under a great monarchy became also a centre of Sanskrit revival.

When the spirit of learning vanished in the north and the Gangetic Valley lay prostrate at the feet of the Turks, the Khiljis and the Tughlaks, the great revival of the Indian mind which gave rise to the Vijayanagar Empire also witnessed a unique revival of Sanskrit. One has only to mention the name of Sayana, the unequalled commentator of the *Vedas,* and his brother Madhavacharya, the author of *Parasara Madhava,* both ministers of Vijayanagar, to indicate the quality of this revival. In the field of letters, Ganga Devi, the author of *Madhura Vijayam* and Varadambika Devi and numerous others bear witness to the close connection of Sanskrit with the revival of national sentiment.

Even in the Moghul Court where, with Akbar, a general feeling of prosperity and well-being returned, the revival of Sanskrit was a remarkable feature. It was under the patronage of Todar Mal, Akbar's Revenue Minister, that the great encyclopaedia of ethics and law, *Todarananda*, was produced. Kavindracharya and Narasimha Bharati, perhaps the greatest scholars of their time, were honoured at the court of the great Moghul, while in the time of Shah Jehan, Jagannath Pandita, the author of *Ganga Lahari*, was given exceptional honours. This general revival of the Hindu mind following the sense of national greatness was reflected in the extraordinary growth of Sanskrit scholarship in Banaras which under Nanda Pandita, Mitra Misra and Nilakanta Bhatta cast its rays far and wide all over India.

On a close examination it will be seen that the Hindu Reformation and the national movement in the 19th and the first half of the 20th century had their best equally in a revival of Sanskrit. True, the earliest authors of this revival were not Indians but Western scholars. It was they who recovered much of India's past through an intensive study of Sanskrit, edited the texts and brought the new methods of scholarship to bear on Sanskrit studies. The result of their activities was an unusually widespread interest in Sanskrit studies in India itself which may be seen in the growing number of research institutions connected with Indology, in the great interest shown in the collection and preservation of ancient books, in the publication of rare manuscripts from many centres all over India, notably in Travancore, Mysore, Baroda and Poona.

Another contribution of European scholarship to Sanskrit and indirectly to our national growth is the emphasis on the international character of Sanskrit. It is mainly due to the work of European scholars in China, Indonesia, Siam, Annam and Cambodia that we know and can take pride in the wide prevalence of Sanskrit as a language of international culture in the Far East. Who will today deny an honoured place in Sanskrit literature to the Prashastis of the Cambodian Kings? An inscription of the time of Yashovarman of Cambodia speaks of him as a greater King than Pravarasena for his Setubandha, a Gunadhya who does not like Prakrit, a Vishalaksha who is opposed to niti, a Sura who humiliated Bhimaka, etc. Among the Prashasti literature of the Java Kings, that of Erlangga Dewa is undoubtedly a gem of Sanskrit poetry, comparable in every way with Harishena's Prashasti on Samudragupta. But more than even the quality of pure Sanskrit writing in many of these inscriptions is the extraordinary and permeating influence which Sanskrit has had on the literature of Java and Siam. The amazing Kakawin literature of Java has a two-fold inspiration, the Epics, *Ramayana* and *Mahabharata*, and the mahakavyas. Thus, for example, *Sumanasantaka* is a mahakavya in Indian Chhandas dealing with the story of Aja and Indumati, clearly based on Kalidasa's *Raghuvamsha*. *Samar Dahana*, anothor elaborate mahakavya in the same language, is again based on the third Sarga of *Kumara Sambhava*. *Arjuna Vivaha* is inspired by Bharavi's *Kiratarjuniya*. It is not necessary to multiply examples. Undeniably, in the period between A.D. 400 and 1200. Sanskrit enjoyed a pre-eminence which was altogether unique. It was widely studied in China and Japan as the translations of numerous Sanskrit classics into the languages of those countries would prove. It was the language of scholarship and culture in Champa (modern Siam), Cambodia, Java, Bali and Sri Vijaya. All these facts which have enabled us to realise the greatness of Sanskrit were discovered by European scholars—Levi, Pelliot, Kern, Stuterhiem and Coedes, so that it may well be claimed that they have contributed a great deal to the present revival of Sanskrit.

If Sanskrit is thus an essential factor of our national life and cannot be separated from it, as I have tried to demonstrate, then it behoves us to ensure that it does not merely remain the embodiment of classical learning, that alongside with making its study popular we should also introduce into it a modern content and give it a new vitality which would absorb all that is of value from other languages. We cannot merely continue to praise Sanskrit for its past greatness and the inspiration that it gives to us. It must live again as a language of culture, as it did at all times of India's national greatness. It must contribute to our life: it must connect itself with the new movements. This is the function of the scholars of today. To this I hope you will devote your attention.

Education in New India

I AM HAPPY to have been afforded this opportunity to take part in your foundation day celebrations and to address you on the occasion. The Central Institute of Education is, I assume, our premier laboratory of education, from where it is hoped new ideas on education will radiate, where new ideals and enthusiasms will be formed, and new methods of teaching and handling youth will be evolved. The need for these will not be questioned by anyone. Society, the world over, is changing; but nowhere is it changing so rapidly as in India. We are, as an independent community, trying to evolve a new life and consequently facing unprecedented problems, whose scope and range we ourselves had not anticipated. We are going through a period of rapid transformation in every aspect of our life, in our social environment no less than in our economic structure, in our spheres of action no less than in the realm of ideas. A casual survey would show how revolutionary these changes have been. In the social field we have witnessed changes which are transforming our age-old institutions, the joint family and the marriage system, the practice of untouchability which by legislation has been abolished and made penal, to mention only a few outstanding instances. In the sphere of economic life we have boldly plunged into a programme of large-scale industrialisation, embarked on a programme of transforming our village communities which already encompasses within its scope over a hundred thousand villages and is intended to cover the whole

Address to the Central Institute of Education, New Delhi, 1955.

of India within the next few years. In our political life we have taken the boldest step of all—entrusted effective power to the entire Indian people by giving the right to vote to every adult man and woman. When it is remembered that about 80 per cent of this immense electorate is illiterate and a large percentage of the whole is living in abject poverty, this transfer of power to the masses will be seen in its true perspective as a revolutionary change of the first magnitude.

In a world which is changing so fast, education, which is naturally a conservative force, must inevitably face a conflict. This is not peculiar to India. So progressive a people as the British, for example, had to reconsider their educational values after the war. The process is a continuous one in the two giants of the modern world, the Soviet Union and America. But nowhere is the problem so emergent as in India, for nowhere was education more official, more directed to the maintenance of the *status quo*, to the discouragement of curiosity and enquiry as in India. That was inevitable. The system of education under the British rule was meant, to a very large extent, to uphold the *status quo*. It was no part of British educational policy in India to encourage curiosity or a sense of intellectual adventure. It was undoubtedly an imposing system that they built up, an all-India educational structure which took but little note of regional differences or variations, enforced a practically uniform curriculum, taught through a common medium. Whatever its weaknesses, and it had many, it is undeniable that it helped to create a common Indian mind; and a reasonable uniformity of standards all over India. Those objectives remain important for us today more than ever. Our national revolt against English as the medium of secondary education, especially on the ground that it confined such education to a small minority, has led to a large-scale regionalisation of secondary education. Practically everywhere high school education is now through the regional languages. This is indeed as it should be. No one at the present time will argue in favour of a return either to English or to the enforcement of Hindi, in non-Hindi areas, as the medium of secondary education. But the problems created by this changeover, especially in the context of the vast changes now taking place, have to be carefully analysed. In the first place there can be no denying the fact that today, in our secondary education, there is no such thing as an all-India standard. Secondly, it is obvious that with the regionalisation of education, the standards themselves have fallen, varying to a great extent with the state of development of the language itself.

This is a point which is generally overlooked. The development of our regional languages in recent years has been remarkable; but it will not be denied that there is a great variation both in the quality and the rate of their development. Some of the languages recognised in the Constitution have, it must be frankly admitted, still to make a great leeway before they can be considered as satisfactory media for education. Naturally, where the language itself is backward, education through it cannot attain the standards which we seek.

When we realise that secondary education is the corner-stone of all national education, that our efficiency as a nation, and our progress in all fields depend on the quality of the secondary school system, it will be realised how basically important it is that the weaknesses which have overtaken us during the transitional period must be rapidly overcome. The Central Government has, I am happy to note, recognised the emergent character of this problem and taken various measures to cope with it. It has brought into existence a Council of Secondary Education, appointed a staff of field officers and has generally laid down policies which are sound enough. These steps may raise efficiency and give to secondary education the central place in our educational structure. But the problem of all-India standards will still remain. Unless we can have an all-India examination as the coping stone of our secondary education, this problem will become a perpetual headache to us. Let me not be misunderstood. I am not suggesting that the local school-leaving certificate or matriculation examinations should be replaced by an all-India examination. They should continue as now, with an additional year of study, as suggested, for purposes of admission to universities. But over and above these local examinations, an all-India examination on the lines of the Cambridge Higher Certificate or the London matriculation examination should be organised, enforcing a uniform and higher standard all over India. Due emphasis can be given to Hindi and English in this examination, and a higher standard for science subjects can be insisted upon. Special schools which exist all over India will prepare boys for this course and even government and private schools in states may in time find it desirable to organise special classes to enable students to sit for it. Those who pass this examination should be entitled to direct admission to technical and scientific institutions and for recruitment to the subordinate Central Services.

In a measure, the Cambridge Senior Certificate Examination is fulfilling this function today. As a result of the higher standards required for this examination and because of its uniformity, it has maintained its popularity even now in the special schools all over the country. What does this prove if not the fact that there is a demand in India in wide circles for a single examination, with uniform standards, all over India? The advantages of such a system are obvious and need not be dilated upon. Apart from ensuring higher standards such an examination will undoubtedly influence education in state schools. It will help to popularise Hindi and maintain at the same time the position of English in our schools and provide a steady supply of students with a better education to our technical institutions.

The fall in standards is also due to our failure to recognise the essential value of examinations. It is not fashionable today to emphasise the necessity of strict and effective written examinations but I am old fashioned enough to think that, far from being a necessary evil, examinations properly conducted are desirable and necessary for a good educational system.

The real functions of a good examination are to distinguish between candidates of different merit, to test the alertness of a candidate's mind, his ability to express himself lucidly and to the point, his capacity to concentrate, and finally to see whether he possesses the minimum knowledge prescribed as the standard for the examination.

Like every institution that human ingenuity invents, there are many patent weaknesses in any system of examination. But so far as I am aware, no one has suggested a suitable alternative. Apart from the question of an alternative method of judgment or an improvement of the present system of examinations, I have not the least doubt in my mind that the standards in education are inseparably bound with the standards of examination. The noticeable fall in our educational standards, which everyone deplores, is in a great measure due to the desire to make examinations more easy in order to facilitate a larger percentage of passes. It may perhaps be too late to raise the standards of regional examinations, but the suggestion which I have put forward of an all-India Higher Certificate Examination may enable us to retrieve some of the lost ground.

The central problem of our education is the fact that, being mainly a product of 19th century ideas, it has not kept up with our political, economic and social progress. We have not co-ordinated it, in any of its aspects, primary, secondary and university, to our fast-changing society. The first real effort to relate it to the new life of our country was by Mahatma Gandhi and his collaborators who evolved the Wardha Scheme. That scheme with necessary modifications still holds the field under the guise of basic education. But its progress has been slow. The exclusive authority of the states in the field of education has stood in the way of its enforcement on a national scale. But the problem does not end there. There must be a continuous examination of educational practice and theory, and adjustments to meet our need.

The magnitude of the problem of education in India is something which is frightening. People are shocked when they hear that only 20 per cent of our population is literate, but they forget that 20 per cent of the Indian population amounts to 72 million people or the combined population of the U. K., Belgium, Holland and Denmark. When it is also remembered that every year the number of children reaching the educational age increases by four and a half millions, one can realise the magnitude of the problem. The race between our increase in population and our ability to provide educational facilities is a close one and will continuously tax our resources and ingenuity. Even if the finance for such a steady annual increase could be provided the major problem of finding qualified teachers would remain with us. This is a basic difficulty with which we are faced. The demand for education is growing. The Constitution places on us the duty of providing everyone with education; but unless we can produce a progressively increasing number of qualified teachers, the problem will remain insoluble.

It is not only a question of man-power, though that is in itself a stupendous problem. Equally it is a question of providing satisfactory conditions of pay and life for the teachers. The salary which we give to our teachers of all grades—but more especially to the primary-school teachers—is a crying scandal. In many states, they hardly get a living wage. The usual reply, and no doubt a valid one, is that state budgets could not bear the burden of any great increase in expenditure and that, in view of the number involved, even a small increase would mean a heavy burden. But whatever the financial arguments, the fact has to be faced that we cannot solve the problem of education unless we provide better pay and living conditions for our teachers.

If the problem of primary education is one of resources and an adequate supply of teachers, the problem of university education is one primarily of quality. Even at the time of the Sadler Commission the problem which they described as revolutionary, of the increasing demand of the middle classes for college education, had become noticeable. Today even the rapid increase in the number of colleges does not keep pace with this ever-increasing demand for admission to universities. The result is the extraordinary and, in my opinion, most unhealthy phenomenon of colleges with four or five thousand students on their roll, where classes are run by shifts, and where the principal is not often acquainted with the members of his own staff. Over thirty-five years ago in a note which C. R. Reddy, a most eminent educationist, submitted to the Mysore Government, he pleaded for smaller universities with an optimum membership of three thousand students, pointing out that some of the best-known universities at the time, like Oxford and Cambridge, did not encourage a much larger number, and how some of the more efficient universities in America also limited their membership. But in India private colleges have in some cases numbers exceeding the total membership of great universities. Nothing in my opinion has been more disastrous to the quality of our university education than this overcrowding in colleges. Just consider for one moment what such an overcrowding involves. Unavoidably, there will be no academic atmosphere in the college. The students can have no common life. They can only be herded into class-rooms and the teaching, even if the teachers are good, cannot be of high quality. Personal contact between the teacher and the student has to be extremely limited. In fact the colleges are reduced to the position of factories—even worse, because no good factory can be run efficiently without satisfactory personal relations between the management and labour. Is it to be wondered at that, over large areas in India, student indiscipline has become very much of an intractable menace, and that the standards of instruction have fallen? Left to themselves, without any kind of direction from their teachers or any kind of loyalty to their colleges, the student community falls a prey to all kinds of influences among which the desire for study becomes perhaps the least important.

Every college steadily tends to become a mammoth institution. In fact a kind of rivalry seems to have come into existence between colleges about their size. The larger the number in a college, the greater it would seem is its prestige. In fact it should be the opposite. Some of the best colleges at Oxford or Cambridge have a very limited membership. The Haverford College, a most remarkable institution with the status of a University, which I once visited had then only a total membership of 1500, a fact in which the authorities took great pride. It was a genuine educational community with a very high academic standard, and justly proud of the contribution it was making to national life in America.

The problem of the overcrowding in colleges cannot be solved by half-hearted measures. It is becoming daily more intractable because the number of those desiring college education keeps on increasing by leaps and bounds, while the facilities which the state and community are able to provide do not increase proportionately. The result is the establishment of mushroom colleges, inadequately staffed and working under intolerable conditions. Many solutions have been suggested, the most important of which is the improvement of secondary education to make it, so to say, self-sufficient, to enable a considerable percentage of students to be diverted directly to technical and professional institutions and also in the hope that the secondary education provided will be of a sufficiently high standard to enable the vast majority to start their life without going through a university education. While it may be possible to divert students from the secondary school direct to technical and professional schools, I am convinced that the attempt to convert secondary education into something which an ordinary man will be satisfied with as giving him the *imprimatur* of a good education will not succeed in India, at least for a considerable time to come. The German and French tradition of the Hoch Schule and the Lycee preparing candidates for direct specialisation in professional schools is not quite applicable to our conditions because of the college tradition which the British introduced and which became attractive because of the degree with which a candidate was rewarded at the end. The attraction of a B. A. or any other degree, which in the popular mind is the passport not merely to appointments, but for being considered an educated man, is too deep-rooted in India to be eliminated by these methods. Unless at the end of our extended secondary school education the student comes out with a degree, with letters after his name, the pressure on our colleges will not only continue but increase. It will take at least two generations before this psychology, not only of the students but of the parents, can be changed.

All the solutions which have been advanced to deal with this problem have as their object the limitation of the number of students seeking admission. This it will be remembered is not a new approach. This was the objective that Lord Curzon had over fifty years ago and his proposals in this connection met with violent opposition on the ground that they were motivated by a desire to deny higher education to Indians. Since then, the problem has only become much more complicated. The recent tendency to substitute regional languages as the medium of college education will greatly increase the magnitude of the problem and unless we can find a suitable remedy at this stage, it will, I am afraid, become insoluble.

This is only one aspect of our growing difficulties in the educational field. To find suitable teaching staff for our colleges has become almost impossible. Recently I have had a most illuminating experience of interviewing a large number of lecturers in colleges who were aspirants for admission to research scholarships. The raw graduates from the universities, though often lacking in a sound educational background, were intelligent and keen but the quality of the lecturers, mostly from private colleges, was a painful revelation. Whatever brightness or keenness they had in their student days had in most cases disappeared. The years they had spent as lecturers had not widened their horizon or added to their intellectual equipment. They seemed never to have felt the thrill of studying something outside the textbooks they had to teach, the exhilaration of assimilating a new experience in the realm of ideas or the sense of adventure of wandering into new fields of thought; in fact most of them had no awareness of anything outside the very narrow field of their daily work. The fault is not theirs. These young men when they left their colleges must have been considered as being among the best of their year, must have obtained high degrees and must have entertained great hopes. What is it that transformed them into dull and often unintelligent lecturers? It is, I am satisfied, the general conditions of their service. In most colleges they are paid a miserable pittance.

In a society dominated by hierarchical conceptions, based on office and salary, their status is low; they are greatly overworked and have to live under very difficult conditions. Naturally their hopes are blasted, and they carry on the teaching profession, not with any sense of vocation, but as a not very pleasant way of earning a meagre livelihood. If the conditions of life of the lecturers in the colleges are not materially improved, there is, I am afraid, no prospect whatever of any improvement in our academic standards.

This is not as easy as it sounds for, if we have to keep pace with the increasing demand for admission to colleges, it is not possible to control or limit private agencies without creating an educational crisis in the country. In spite of all our national effort, the private colleges, established as a result of non-official activity, and often motivated by high philanthropic considerations, have to bear much of the burden of expansion. Today they fulfil a national need and, in a country so poor as India, it is impossible to lay down rigid conditions if we are to encourage private effort in the field of education. This is the dilemma we face.

It is not only the question of pay that is important. It is also the question of status. The bureaucratic tradition of the British Indian administration gave an artificial and altogether undeserved glamour to executive services under the government. Even a university professor, unless he had achieved a very special personal position, was a minor fry compared to an obscure official. It is said of a very distinguished professor in one of the colleges in the South that when as a result of unusual distinction in his M. A. examination he was appointed straightaway as an Assistant Professor in one of the leading colleges, on a respectable salary, his aged father was greatly distressed that he had not even secured the post of a police sub-inspector. This attitude is not unusual even now. The prestige of officialdom is a blasting factor in the growth of our national life. It has had two results, both of which can only be considered as harmful from the national point of view. The most-qualified young men choose government service even in minor capacities rather than positions in colleges and universities; and secondly it gives to the teaching profession an unnecessary feeling of inferiority. Recently I had attached to me on deputation from government a junior officer who was a very promising historian, the author of a notable piece of research and desirous still of continuing his work in that field. When his period of deputation with me was coming to a close, I asked him why he did not choose an educational career as he was still young and enthusiastic and I offered to help him to find a readership in some university. His reply was very frank. He said that when he reverted to his substantive post he would receive a salary which was at least twice that of a reader and higher than the starting salary of a professor. The scales, he said, are weighted too heavily against such a choice. Besides there was the question of status. So, reluctantly, he chose to go back to the files hoping to continue to do some research in his leisure moments.

A significant fact, illustrating the high status which academic work enjoys in countries like England, is the number of cases of people returning to the universities after holding very high political appointments. I need mention only two very notable instances. The late Herbert Fisher, the historian, when I first knew him, was a teaching Fellow of New College. During the first Great War, he became a member of the government and even held charge for a time of the post of Secretary of State for India. After the war, he returned to history and gave to the world his *History of Europe* in three volumes and was later elected Warden of New College. A more recent instance is that of Lord Cherwell, who was one of the key figures in the War Cabinet of Churchill, a person of the highest influence in the determination of national policies. After the war, he quietly returned to his teaching work at Oxford. When I last met him, this great statesman was sitting in perfect contentment in the senior common room at Christ Church, discussing college affairs with other dons.

The profession of teaching in universities is held in such high honour in England that Cabinet Ministers at the height of their influence do not disdain to return to it. To expect such a thing in India would perhaps be aiming too high, but we could at least raise the status of our teachers that they need not feel that, compared to government officials, they are mere nobodies.

All these maladjustments in regard to education and indeed even the inefficiency of the system can be traced to the irrational organisation of our society. Good education, says one of our own great educational thinkers, cannot pull its weight except in a good society, that is a justly and rationally planned society. No one, I am sure, will deny this obvious fact. In a society which is ill-organised, without purposive direction, and uninfluenced by high ideals, education will always be haphazard, inefficient, and incapable of creating the sense of mental, moral and physical discipline which should be one of the primary objects of education. The state of our education is only one aspect of the many-sided *malaise* from which our society is suffering—the indiscipline of our national life. The inefficiency and lack of direction in our educational system is only an aspect of our own national inefficiency and the lack of social direction in our life. If the teachers in our educational institutions do not enjoy the status and position which they should enjoy, it is because of the false values which have come to dominate our society. The problem of the improvement of our education is, therefore, to my mind, a part of the wider problem of finding a basic solution for our social *malaise*. This, of course, does not mean that we should not attempt to deal with the problem from the educational point of view and correct the more obvious evils. It is to that question that our efforts should now be directed.

A democratic society must believe in youth and necessarily it must believe in education. It is obvious that without popular education democracy cannot function, and the popular education of today must meet the needs of the community in all its varied aspects. It must provide for every educated man and woman to have an understanding of national values, of the main trends of our history and political institutions. It must also be adjusted to the ranges of individual ability. An education that enables us to live in our ivory towers may have its uses, but it will not serve national purposes today for, essentially, it will be a class education, with but little relation to the realities of our life.

Education is too important a matter for our national life for it to be made the plaything of people who have not devoted time and thought to it. It is only in an institution like this Central Institute of Education that the work of thinking out the new problems of education can be undertaken and I have no doubt that it was founded with that object in view. It is my prayer that you may live up to that ideal and serve the cause of education in India.

The Population Problem in India

I AM GLAD to inaugurate the Indian Institute for Population Studies. It is the only one of its kind in India and, so far as I know, the only one of its kind in Asia, outside Japan. Indeed the science itself is not very old, and though a little consideration will show how important it is in a modern society, it is still in a state of infancy in India, where universities and other institutions of learning, following the classical traditions of England, have given but little attention to it.

Population has always been one of the major factors of history. It is the movement of people either in search of grazing grounds in the broad plains and steppes of Central Asia or forced forward by the pressure of more dynamic groups that created the civilisation of the Gangetic Valley.

The great wandering of peoples, the Huns, the Goths and the Mongols, which changed the face of Europe and Asia over the centuries cannot be explained, as it used to be by earlier historians, as scourges of God or as visitations of the Apocalypse, but as resulting from the pressure of economic problems on a mobile population. The great expansion of European peoples in the New Hemisphere, in portions of Africa and in Australasia, which is perhaps the most significant demographic change during the last three hundred years, and the great transformation which is taking place before our very eyes, converting the wild and dreary steppes of Siberia into flourishing industrial areas, fast developing into great centres

Address inaugurating the Indian Institute for Population Studies, Annamalainagar, 1950 of population, will shape the course of history for thousands of years to come. What geological shifts in civilisation these movements of people involve may easily be conceived when we look at the racial and cultural composition of the world now and compare it with the position a hundred years ago.

Though the problems connected with population are thus fundamental, their scientific study is of recent origin. Its immense significance came like a flash to an English parson who was deeply concerned with the tremendous growth of population in England following the Industrial Revolution and the apparent inability of the English acreage to provide food for its inhabitants. Before the Industrial Revolution England was self-supporting in food-grains. With the tremendous increase in her population which the new industries brought in their wake, the little island was unable to provide adequate food supplies. This is the problem that faced Malthus, whose theory of the ratio of increase in population and food fell like a thunderbolt on the glowing optimism of the 19th century. In its essentials the Malthusian theory was simple. It postulated that population increased by geometrical progression and had no limits, and that so far as food was concerned its production increased only at a much lower rate and had definite limits owing to the area of cultivation available to men. The theory was branded as pessimistic. Certainly the history of the century that has passed since Malthus enunciated his theory seemed to falsify his prophecies. The opening up of new areas, the application of science to agriculture, both for increased production and for preventing the decay of land, and recovering it for use where the law of decreasing returns had begun to operate, and the utilisation of new products seemed to nullify the logic of Malthus. But has the Malthusian doctrine been finally disproved? The claim for living space, which became a national slogan with the most populous nation of Europe, Germany, the insistent demand for territorial cutlets, which Italy, lacking the natural resources of other nations, has put forward ever since she become a united nation; and the pressure of the population on land which drove Japan overseas—all these show that we can shut our eyes to the Malthusian dilemma only at great peril to the future.

In India especially the problem has acquired an urgency which is only now being recognised. In the course of a century the population of India has more than doubled itself. In 1851, it is calculated that India had only 150 million people. According to the census of 1941, the same area had to bear no less than 388 millions. After the secession of the provinces which now constitute Pakistan, the pressure has become even greater. A larger percentage of the grain-growing areas has fallen to the lot of Pakistan. Thus the problem of feeding India's population, which was growing more and more difficult with every passing year that saw an increase of five millions to the population, became suddenly the dominating fact in our life.

It is unnecessary for me to emphasise how overriding this problem of population has become. The very future of our country as a progressive, independent nation now depends on the way we are able to tackle the inter-related problems of food and population.

I have heard it stated often that India is over-populated and that the optimum of population in relation to our food resources has long been reached. Though I can only speak as a layman, it is obvious that the imbalance in our population lies in its spatial distribution. While there are some areas in India, especially the deltaic regions and the Gangetic Valley which are over-populated, there are vast territories in Rajputana, in Central India and even in the Deccan where the density is meagre. Though our food production is now substantially below our requirements, it is well known that many million acres of land await to be reclaimed in India. Also, food experts are dinning into our ears the undoubted fact that our agriculture remains in many ways primitive and yield per acre is the smallest in the world. Clearly, what we require is a population policy which will take into consideration the problems of spatial adjustment and a long-period programme in respect of food production which will bring the abandoned lands under the plough, and also by improved methods change the quality of land and make it yield more. The inexorable logic of facts has forced the Government to take in hand a comprehensive policy with regard to land and production. But the related problem of a population policy, without which we cannot succeed, seems to have been lost sight of.

It is obvious that when our large schemes of irrigation begin to materialise, this problem of the spatial distribution of population will force itself on the Government. Speaking on the basis of some experience of large-scale canal irrigation in Bikaner, I can say without hesitation that the problem of populating the new irrigation colonies with cultivators prepared to put their labour and knowledge into the land will be an extremely difficult one, unless it is planned beforehand. We know for example that lands in Bhawalpur could not be sold for many years after water had become available. In Ganganagar Colony in the state of Bikaner some of the land was taken up only ten years after the irrigation scheme was in operation and these were areas bordering on the Punjab where the people had a long background of farming in irrigated colonies. Our large-scale irrigation schemes, Bhakra, Damodar Valley, Hirakud and Chambal will within a few years begin to supply water, but it is futile to think that people will rush to these areas to buy land and settle down and begin to produce food which we so urgently need. It will be nothing less than political madness to leave these colonies to be filled up haphazard. In the first place, it may take years or even decades before the colonies get fully populated. Secondly, unless it is planned beforehand, land may even go into the hands of speculators and other unproductive clans and the great schemes on which so much depends may not yield us the maximum results.

The urgent necessity for a population policy in India is therefore clear. It will have to be formulated in terms of our industrial and agricultural programmes, with a view both to create a balance and to relieve the strain in areas which are undoubtedly over-populated. The basic problems which we shall have to consider in laying down our policy may briefly be touched upon here. In the first place, we have to relate our population to regional resources, to enquire into and discover the causes for the immobility of our agricultural classes, the social bonds that tie them to particular areas and the factors which may be brought into play to encourage movement among them. Secondly, we have to study the problem in relation to the pressure on land, the food habits and other factors which tend to make our food-population relationship a rigid one. A third aspect of the problem which has also to be studied carefully is the relationship of climatic factors to human energy. It is well known that the moist monsoon belt has the largest density of population, accounting for very nearly a fourth of the human race. It is equally a well-known fact that the population of the monsoon belt is physically the most enervated, comparatively less capable of energy and more subject to diseases. Climatology is an essential branch of the science of population.

There are of course other and better known aspects of the population problem such as fertility and mortality, the curious fact of the under-developed groups being the sources of population increase, the rural-urban differentiation and the possibility of an artificial control of the birth rate. Whether a general ecological law could be evolved out of ascertained facts and whether by the natural operation of social forces the balance of population gets adjusted automatically are also matters for enquiry.

But whether the problem is one of formulating a population policy for a single country or one of discovering general laws, the main difficulty of a country like India lies in establishing a factual groundwork based on detailed study. We have, compared to other countries in Asia, an efficient and comprehensive system of census and I am happy to note that the Census Department is now to be put on a permanent basis, so that the work of collection, classification and statistical analysis can be continuous. But a census provides only the raw material for research. A solution of our problems will become easier only when trained researchers take up different aspects of the problem and study them with scientific accuracy. This is the object with which the Indian Institute for

Population Studies is being founded. It is a matter of satisfaction that Dr. Sripati Chandrasekhar, who is one of the few in India who has studied this subject for many years and written authoritatively on the matter, should have taken the initiative in establishing this Institute at the University. Under his direction this body will, I am sure, attain a position of national eminence by the enthusiasm which he and his students will bring to bear on all aspects of the population question and by the quality of the work which it produces. Dr. Chandrasekhar is to be congratulated especially on having been able to secure the co-operation of the major workers in the field of Indian Economics through a National Executive Committee and an International Advisory Board which includes the names of such outstanding men as Lord Boyd-Orr, Carr Saunders, Alfred Sauvy and Warren Thompson. Their names are more than a guarantee of the scientific status of the Institute, which I trust will receive international recognition as a leading centre of population research. I hope that, recognising its national value, the Government of India, the Provincial Governments and the universities will give it ample support.

In conclusion I should like to congratulate, in the first place, Dr. Chandrasekhar, who has been able even in a modest degree to realise his dreams by the establishment of this Institute and, secondly, the University for the encouragement it has given him in his task.